# IRISH EMIGRANTS IN NORTH AMERICA

## Part Six

by David Dobson

CLEARFIELD

Printed for
Clearfield Company, Inc. by
Genealogical Publishing Co., Inc.
Baltimore, Maryland
2003

International Standard Book Number: 0-8063-5216-7

*Made in the United States of America*

# INTRODUCTION

Emigration from Ireland to the Americas can be said to have started in earnest during the early eighteenth century. In 1718 the first successful emigration from Ireland to New England occurred, which laid the foundations for the large-scale settlement of colonial America by the "Scotch-Irish." There had been groups of Irish settlers during the seventeenth century, some involuntary, in the West Indies. The earliest attempt, albeit unsuccessful, to emigrate from Ireland to New England was that of a group aboard the *Eaglewing* in the 1630s. Some early emigrants went as indentured servants, often via ports such as Bristol and London. The scale of emigration, particularly from the north of Ireland, grew from a trickle in 1718 to a torrent in the mid-nineteenth century. Specific groups of emigrants have attracted the attention of researchers such as Frances McDonnell, who has identified felons and criminals involuntarily transported to America in her Emigrants from Ireland to America 1735-1743 (Baltimore, 1992). Ira Glazier and Michael Tepper list tens of thousands who were forced to seek refuge in America during and after the potato famine 1846-1851 in The Famine Immigrants (Baltimore, 1984-).

Part Six is based mainly on archival sources in Canada, England, Ireland, Scotland and the United States, together with contemporary newspapers and journals, a few published records and some gravestone inscriptions from both sides of the Atlantic.

David Dobson
St Andrews, Scotland, 2003.

# IRISH EMIGRANTS IN NORTH AMERICA,
## Part Six

**ABBOT, JEREMIAH,** born 1798, from Rathcormick, County Cork, emigrated from Cove on the <u>Stakesby</u> to Quebec on 8 July 1823, settled in Lanark, Ontario. [PAO.prp]

**ACRES, THOMAS,** from Ireland, settled in March, Ontario, on 29 October 1820. [PAO.MS154]

**AGNUE, WILLIAM,** from Ireland, settled in Goulburn, Ontario, on 25 June 1822. [PAO.MS154]

**AHAGH, CATHERINE,** from Youghal to Maryland on the <u>Encrease of Youghal</u>, master Philip Popplestone, in 1679. [Dorchester Co. Patents, WC#129] [MSA.Patents#20/184]

**AHERN, JOHN,** born 1795, with wife Bridget born 1796 – who died 29 July 1823, and children Thomas born 1820 and Jane born 1821, from Castletownroche, County Cork, emigrated from Cove on the <u>Stakesby</u> to Quebec on 8 July 1823, settled in Pakenham, Ontario. [PAO.prp]

**AIRES, JOHN,** from Ireland, settled in Huntley, Ontario, on 20 May 1821. [PAO.MS154]

**ALEXANDER, JAMES,** from Waterford on the <u>St George of London</u>, to Maryland in 1677. [SPDom#19/393][MSA.LO.Patents#15/553]

**ALEXANDER, RICHARD,** from Ireland, settled in Monaghan, Newcastle, Ontario, on 2 May 1818. [PAO.MS154]

**ALLAN, AUGUSTUS,** from Ireland, a former private of the 4th Veteran Battalion, settled in Beckwith, Ontario, on 9 September 1817. [PAO.MS154]

**ALLAN, SAMUEL,** a surgeon from Ireland, settled in Smith, Newcastle, Ontario, on 12 December 1819. [PAO.MS154]

**ALLAY, BARNABY,** born 1704, an Irish indentured servant who absconded from John Quarles at King William Court House, Virginia, on 10 October 1754. [VaGaz.7.11.1754]

**ALPIN, JAMES,** from Ireland, a former sergeant of the 10$^{TH}$ Regiment, settled in Bathurst, Ontario, on 2 October 1817. [PAO.MS154]

**ANDERSON, JOHN,** probably from the parish of Billy in County Antrim, settled in Philadelphia by 1837. [PRONI#D1828/7]

**ANDERSON, JOSEPH,** from Ballinrees, parish of Aghadowey, County Londonderry, settled in West Salem, Mercer County, Pennsylvania, by 1840. [PRONI#T2294/1]

**ARGUE, GEORGE,** from Ireland, settled in Goulburn, Ontario, on 20 November 1821. [PAO.MS154]

**ARGUE, THOMAS,** from Ireland, settled in Huntley, Ontario, on 23 August 1820. [PAO.MS154]

**ARMSTRONG, ANDREW,** a cooper from Ireland, settled in Cavan, Newcastle, Ontario, on 20 October 1818. [PAO.MS154]

**ARMSTRONG, ANDREW,** from Ireland, settled in Cavan, Newcastle, Ontario, on 3 March 1819. [PAO.MS154]

**ARMSTRONG, CHARLES,** from Ireland, settled in Cavan, Ontario, on 9 September 1817. [PAO.MS154]

**ARMSTRONG, DAVID,** from Ireland, settled in Cavan, Newcastle, Ontario, on 9 September 1817. [PAO.MS154]

**ARMSTRONG, JAMES,** a former private of the 70$^{th}$ Regiment, with his wife, son and 2 daughters, land grant in Bathurst, Ontario, on 2 September 1819. [PAO.MS154]

**ARMSTRONG, JAMES,** from Ireland, settled in March, Ontario, on 26 January 1821. [PAO.MS154]

**ARMSTRONG, JOHN,** from Ireland, settled in Cavan, Ontario, on 9 September 1817. [PAO.MS154]

**ARMSTRONG, JOHN,** from Ireland, settled in Huntley, Ontario, on 18 September 1822. [PAO.MS154]

**ARMSTRONG, JOHN,** a yeoman from Ireland, settled in Toronto, Home, Ontario, on 22 April 1819. [PAO.MS154]

**ARMSTRONG, ROBERT,** from Ireland, settled in Huntley, Ontario, on 30 May 1822. [PAO.MS154]

**ARMSTRONG, ROBERT,** with Margaret, Jane, Janny, Sophia, Rebecca, Elizabeth and Thomas, from

Kilfinnane, County Limerick, emigrated from the Cove
of Cork on the Hebe bound for Quebec on 8 July 1823,
settled in Ramsay, Ontario. [PAO.prp]

**ARMSTRONG, THOMAS,** and his wife, landed from the
Consonby on 24 July 1821, settled in Beckwith,
Ontario, on 4 December 1821. [PAO.MS154]

**ARMSTRONG, WILLIAM**, with his wife, two sons and seven
daughters, from Ireland, landed from the Atlantic on 14
August 1817, settled in Landsdowne, Ontario, on 13
October 1817. [PAO.MS154]

**ARMSTRONG, WILLIAM,** from Ireland, settled in Cavan,
Ontario, on 9 September 1817. [PAO.MS154]

**ARONEY, JAMES,** an indentured servant, who emigrated
from Belfast on the Bruerton of Liverpool, master John
Fowler, to Philadelphia in 1729. [PRONI#D354/71]

**ARTHUR, ANTHONY,** from Waterford on the St George of
London, to Maryland in 1677.
[SPDom#19/393][MSA.LO.Patents#15/553]

**ASHBILL, DAVID,** born 1716, 6 feet tall, an Irish  indentured
servant  who absconded from Robert Vaulx in
Westmoreland County, Virginia, in 1751.
[VaGaz.2.5.1751]

**ASHWOOD, RICHARD**, from Youghal to Maryland on the
Encrease of Youghal, master Philip Popplestone, in
1679. [Dorchester Co. Patents, WC#129]
[MSA.Patents#20/184]

**ATHERTON, THOMAS**, from Ireland, purchased land in
West New Jersey, 1664. [NYGBR#30]

**ATKINSON, NICHOLAS,** a merchant in Grenada 1770. [NLI]

**AVERY, JOSEPH,** from Ireland, formerly a corporal of the
104th Regiment, with his wife, son and daughter, settled
in Bathurst, Ontario, 30 January 1818. [PAO.MS154]

**AYLRED, JOHN,** a merchant from Waterford, in
Newfoundland around 1676. [PRO.CO1/38.{1676}, 39]

**BAILEY, GEORGE,** sr., from Ireland, settled in Beckwith,
Ontario, on 25 January 1820. [PAO.MS154]

**BAILEY, GEORGE,** jr., from Ireland, settled in Beckwith,
Ontario, on 30 January 1820. [PAO.MS154]

**BAILEY, THOMAS,** born 1750, from northern Ireland, settled
in Maryland before 1772, Loyalist. [PRO.AO12.99.120]

**BAKER, JOHN,** from Waterford on the <u>St George of London</u>, to Maryland in 1677.
[SPDom#19/393][MSA.LO.Patents#15/553]

**BAKER, WILLIAM,** from Waterford on the <u>St George of London</u>, to Maryland in 1677.
[SPDom#19/393][MSA.LO.Patents#15/553]

**BARRET, JEAN,** born 1725, an Irish indentured servant, absconded from John Lawson, Fork of Gunpowder, Baltimore County, Maryland, on 24 September 1745.
[MdGaz#27]

**BARRETT, RICHARD,** born by 1700, a carpenter and indentured servant who absconded from John Bordley and Kinvin Wroth in Chester Town, Maryland, on August 1752. [MdGaz#386]

**BARRY, JANE,** from Waterford on the <u>St George of London</u>, to Maryland in 1677.
[SPDom#19/393][MSA.LO.Patents#15/553]

**BARRY, JOHN,** born 1791, with Fanny born 1804, from Mallow, County Cork, emigrated from Cove on the <u>Stakesby</u> to Quebec on 8 July 1823, settled in Ramsay township, Ontario. [PAO.prp]

**BARRY, MARY,** from Waterford on the <u>St George of London</u>, to Maryland in 1677.
[SPDom#19/393][MSA.LO.Patents#15/553]

**BARTON, BENJAMIN,** from Ireland, settled in Huntley, Ontario, on 30 October 1822. [PAO.MS154]

**BAYLEY, MARGARET,** from Dublin to North Carolina on the <u>George of Dublin,</u> master Thomas Cumming, in 1735.
[ICJ]

**BEAL, BENJAMIN,** from Ireland, settled in Goulburn, Ontario, on 31 July 1822. [PAO.MS154]

**BEAMISH, WILLIAM,** from Ireland, settled in Cavan, Newcastle, Ontario, on 10 May 1818. [PAO.MS154]

**BEARD, THOMAS,** born 1742, Nancy born 1743, Mary born 1763, and Martha born 1764, arrived in South Carolina in January 1768 on the brigantine <u>Chichester,</u> master William Reid, from Belfast. [SCCJ.34.1]

**BEATTIE, DANIEL,** from Ireland, settled in March, Ontario, on 23 August 1820. [PAO.MS154]

**BEATTIE, DAVID,** a yeoman from Ireland, settled in Toronto, Home, Ontario, on 22 April 1819. [PAO.MS154]

**BEATTIE, JAMES,** a yeoman from Ireland, settled in Toronto, Home, Ontario, on 22 April 1819. [PAO.MS154]

**BEATTIE, ROBERT,** from Ireland, settled in Cavan, Newcastle, Ontario, on 14 October 1817. [PAO.MS154]

**BEATTY, JOHN,** Afrom Ireland, settled in Toronto, Home, Ontario, on 22 April 1819. [PAO.MS154]

**BEATTY, PATRICK,** from Ireland, settled in Goulburn, Ontario, on 6 March 1822. [PAO.MS154]

**BELL, ISABELL,** born 1727, Elizabeth born 1747, John born 1750, William born 1751, and Mary born 1762, arrived in South Carolina in January 1768 on the brigantine Chichester, master William Reid, from Belfast. [SCCJ.34.1]

**BELL, SARAH,** born 1719, with John born 1748, and Sarah born 1746, emigrated from Belfast on the Chichester, a brigantine, master William Reid, arrived in Charleston, South Carolina, on 25 December 1767. [SCGaz]

**BENJAMIN, JAMES,** sr., arrived on the Satham, 7 August 1817, land grant in Edwardsburgh, Ontario, 1 February 1818. [PAO.MS154]

**BENNET, ELIZABETH,** born in Ireland during 1811, settled in Caledon, Peel County, Ontario, died on 26 January 1891. [Caledon g/s]

**BENNET, JAMES,** from Ireland, settled in Cavan, Newcastle, Ontario, on 9 September 1817. [PAO.MS154]

**BENSON, JOHN,** born 1791, wife Mary born 1795, and children William born 1816, Francis born 1818, Robert born 1820, and John born 1822, from Charleville, County Cork, emigrated from Cove on the Stakesby to Quebec on 8 July 1823, settled in Ramsay township, Ontario. [PAO.prp]

**BENSON, THOMAS,** an Irish indentured servant, 5 feet 9 inches tall, absconded from Nathan Morgan, Neck Creek, Fincastle, Virginia, in 1775. [VaGaz.30.6.1775]

**BERNEY, WILLIAM,** with his wife, three sons and four daughters, from Ireland, landed from the Mary Ann on 8 August 1817, settled in Kitley, Ontario, on 16 September 1817. [PAO.MS154]

**BERRY, JOHN,** an Irish indentured servant who absconded from James Toone in Richmond County, Virginia, on 7 July 1738. [VaGaz.15.9.1738]

**BERTRAM, JOHN,** from Ireland, settled in Lanark, Ontario, on 25 April 1822. [PAO.MS154]

**BIRCH, GEORGE,** from Ireland, settled in Goulburn, Ontario, on 2 November 1822. [PAO.MS154]

**BIRCH, THOMAS,** from Ireland, settled in Goulburn, Ontario, on 2 November 1822. [PAO.MS154]

**BIRK, JOHN,** born in Ireland, 5 feet 8 inches tall, a convict-indentured servant who absconded from Richard Graham in Dumfries, Virginia, during April 1759. [MdGaz#733]

**BISE, JOHN,** from Waterford on the St George of London, to Maryland in 1677. [SPDom#19/393][MSA.LO.Patents#15/553]

**BLACK, EDWARD,** from Ireland, settled in Ramsay, Ontario, on 6 May1821. [PAO.MS154]

**BLACKBURN, GEORGE,** with his wife, two sons and four daughters, from Ireland, settled in Lanark, Ontario, on 22 October 1821. [PAO.MS154]

**BLACKSTOCK, MOSES,** a yeoman from Ireland, settled in Cavan, Newcastle, Ontario, on 12 September 1818. [PAO.MS154]

**BLAIR, JAMES,** in St Eustatia, 1780-1795. [PRONI#DOD.717/19-27]

**BLAIR, JAMES,** from Ireland, settled in Goulburn, Ontario, on 29 November 1821. [PAO.MS154]

**BLAIR, Captain JOHN,** born in County Tyrone during 1770, died in Yorkville, South Carolina, on 3 October 1848. [Lincolnton Courier: 28.10.1848]

**BLAIR, THOMAS,** a merchant from Dublin, probate 27 February 1767 New York

**BLASHFORD, MICHAEL,** an Irish convict indentured servant who absconded from Richard Arell in Alexandria, Virginia, on 6 May 1771. [VaGaz.23.5.1771]

**BLEEX, THOMAS,** from Ireland, settled in Goulburn, Ontario, on 29 September 1820. [PAO.MS154]

**BLOOMER, JOHN,** formerly a private of the 8th Regiment, from Ireland, settled in Burgess, Ontario, on 22 August 1816. [PAO.MS154]

**BODEL, WILLIAM,** born 1821, son of Robert and Rebecca Bodel, died in New Orleans during July 1853. [Drumbo g/s, County Down]

**BONNY, RICHARD,** from Waterford on the St George of London, to Maryland in 1677.
[SPDom#19/393][MSA.LO.Patents#15/553]

**BOOTH, ROBERT,** from Ireland, settled in Huntley, Ontario, on 30 October 1822. [PAO.MS154]

**BORROUS, ANN,** an indentured servant who emigrated from Limerick to America on the Industry of Westhaven, master James Lowes, in March 1774. [Hook pp, DU]

**BOUCHIER, JOHN,** from Ireland, settled in March, Ontario, on 23 August 1820. [PAO.MS154]

**BOURK, WILLIAM,** an Irish indentured servant and sawyer who absconded from LeRoy Griffin, in Richmond County, Virginia, on 23 April 1737. [VaGaz.13.5.1737]

**BOURKE, EDWARD,** from Youghal to Maryland on the Encrease of Youghal, master Philip Popplestone, in 1679. [Dorchester Co. Patents, WC#129]
[MSA.Patents#20/184]

**BOWEN, MARY,** from Youghal to Maryland on the Encrease of Youghal, master Philip Popplestone, in 1679. [Dorchester Co. Patents, WC#129]
[MSA.Patents#20/184]

**BOWING, EDMUND,** a shoemaker and indentured servant, absconded from Isaac Lee, Cambridge, Dorchester County, Maryland, on 20 June 1748. [MdGaz#169]

**BOWMAN, ANDREW,** from Ireland, was naturalised in Stokes County, North Carolina, on 22 April 1809. [NCSA.CR.090/3111/1]

**BOYDE, JOHN,** born 1742, and Nancy born 1747, arrived in South Carolina in January 1768 on the brigantine Chichester, master William Reid, from Belfast. [SCCJ.34.1]

**BOYLE, HENRY,** born 1803, from Clonmeen, County Clare, emigrated from Cove on the Stakesby to Quebec on 8 July 1823, settled in Pakenham, Ontario. [PAO.prp]

**BOYLE, THOMAS,** born 1793, with wife Mary born 1791, and children William born 1815, mary born 1818, Charles born 1819, and esther born 1822, from Clonmeen, County Clare, emigrated from Cove on the Stakesby to Quebec on 8 July 1823, settled in Pakenham, Ontario. [PAO.prp]

**BOYLE, WILLIAM,** emigrated from Portrush on the Providence, master Thomas Clark, 27 August 1768, bound for New York, shipwrecked on 8 September 1768. [BNL#3283:3.2.1769]

**BRADBURN, GEORGE,** a yeoman from Ireland, settled in Cavan, Newcastle, Ontario, on 9 September 1818. [PAO.MS154]

**BRADBURN, JOHN,** a yeoman from Ireland, settled in Cavan, Newcastle, Ontario, on 9 September 1818. [PAO.MS154]

**BRADBURN, THOMAS,** a tailor from Ireland, settled in Cavan, Newcastle, Ontario, on 15 October 1818. [PAO.MS154]

**BRADLEY, DAVID,** an indentured servant, emigrated from Belfast on the Bruerton of Liverpool, master John Fowler, to Philadelphia in 1729. [PRONI#D354/71]

**BRADLEY, JOHN,** from Ireland, settled in Huntley, Ontario, on 30 November 1821. [PAO.MS154]

**BRADLEY, MATHEW,** an indentured servant, emigrated from Belfast on the Bruerton of Liverpool, master John Fowler, to Philadelphia in 1729. [PRONI#D354/71]

**BRANNAN, JOHN,** from Ireland, settled in Goulburn, Ontario, on 5 March 1822. [PAO.MS154]

**BREADON, JOHN,** from Ireland, settled in Cavan, Newcastle, Ontario, on 5 October 1818. [PAO.MS154]

**BREAKEY, ANDREW,** from Ireland, settled in Cavan, Newcastle, Ontario, on 5 October 1818. [PAO.MS154]

**BREATON, THOMAS,** born 1751, 5 feet 9 inches tall, an Irish indentured servant who absconded from John Clifford near Alexandria, Prince George County, Virginia, on 27 August 1774. [VaGaz.1.9.1774]

**BRENDEVILL, JOHN,** from Youghal to Maryland on the Encrease of Youghal, master Philip Popplestone, in 1679. [Dorchester Co. Patents, WC#129] [MSA.Patents#20/184]

**BRESNEHAN, MAURICE,** born 1799, from Buttevant, County Cork, emigrated from Cove on the Stakesby to Quebec on 8 July 1823, settled in Ramsay township, Ontario. [PAO.prp]

**BREWER, JAMES,** an indentured servant, emigrated from Belfast on the Bruerton of Liverpool, master John Fowler, to Philadelphia in 1729. [PRONI#D354/71]

**BRIGGS, STANLEY,** jr., with his wife, landed from the Sisters on 26 June 1821, settled in Bathurst, Ontario, on 3 December 1821. [PAO.MS154]

**BRITT, JOHN,** from Waterford on the St George of London, to Maryland in 1677.
[SPDom#19/393][MSA.LO.Patents#15/553]

**BRITT, JOHN,** born 1750, 5 feet 8 inches tall, an Irish indentured servant who absconded from Samuel Arell in Alexandria, Prince George County, Virginia, on 15 December 1776. [VaGaz.27.121776]

**BROTHERS, DAVIS,** from Youghal to Maryland on the Encrease of Youghal, master Philip Popplestone, in 1679. [Dorchester Co. Patents, WC#129] [MSA.Patents#20/184]

**BROTHY, DENNIS,** from Waterford on the St George of London, to Maryland in 1677.
[SPDom#19/393][MSA.LO.Patents#15/553]

**BROWN, ALEXANDER,** from Ireland, settled in Cavan, Newcastle, Ontario, on 12 May 1818. [PAO.MS154]

**BROWN, ARTHUR,** born 1699 in Droghera, son of Reverend John B. Brown, sent to Providence, New England, on 12 November 1729. [EMA#17]

**BROWN, DANIEL,** an indentured servant who emigrated from Belfast on the Bruerton of Liverpool, master John Fowler, to Philadelphia in 1729. [PRONI#D354/71]

**BROWN, JAMES,** from Shercock, Ireland, settled in Cavan, Newcastle, Ontario, on 15 September 1817. [PAO.MS154]

**BROWN, JAMES,** born 1804, from Lismore, County Waterford, emigrated from Cove on the Stakesby to Quebec on 8 July 1823, settled in Ramsay township, Ontario. [PAO.prp]

**BROWN, JOHN,** born in Belfast, formerly a merchant in Dublin, captured by the French when on passage for

Antigua, died on Mari Galante Island, West Indies, in September 1808. [GM#78/1126]

BROWN, JOHN, emigrated from County Tyrone to Quebec in 1819. [PRONI.T3102.1.12]

BROWN, JOHN, settled in Beckwith, Ontario, on 2 May 1821. [PAO.MS154]

BROWN, JOHN, probably from the parish of Billy, County Antrim, settled near Philadelphia by 1837. [PRONI#D1828/7]

BROWN, NEILL, born 1723, from Belfast, settled in Fog's Manor, Chester County, Pennsylvania, Loyalist, returned to Ireland. [PRO.AO12.102.135]

BROWN, SAMUEL, emigrated from Belfast to Philadelphia in 1793. [PRONI#T3525]

BROWN, WILLIAM, sr., from Ireland, settled in Huntley, Ontario, on 6 September 1822. [PAO.MS154]

BROWN, WILLIAM, jr., from Ireland, settled in Huntley, Ontario, on 18 September 1817. [PAO.MS154]

BROWN, WILLIAM, born 1807, from Lismore, County Waterford, emigrated from Cove on the Stakesby to Quebec on 8 July 1823, settled in Ramsay township, Ontario. [PAO, prp]

BROWNE, JAMES, from Ireland, settled in Cavan, Ontario, on 9 September 1817. [PAO.MS154]

BROWNLEE, ALEXANDER, emigrated from Ireland to Canada, settled in Goulburn, Ontario, on 30 March 1820. [PAO, MS154]

BROWNLEE, JAMES, sr., from Ireland, settled in Goulburn, Ontario, on 10 August 1821. [PAO.MS154]

BROWNLEE, ROBERT, from Ireland, settled in Goulburn, Ontario, on 30 August 1821. [PAO.MS154]

BROWNLEE, WILLIAM, from Ireland, settled in Goulburn, Ontario, on 10 August 1821. [PAO.MS154]

BRYAN, CORNELIUS, an Irish servant in Barbados, 1656. [Minutes of the Council of Barbados, 15.1.1656]

BRYAN, HONOR, from Waterford on the St George of London, to Maryland in 1677. [SPDom#19/393][MSA.LO.Patents#15/553]

BRYAN, JOHN, from Ireland, a former private of the 51st Regiment, with his wife, two sons and one daughter,

settled in Drummond, Ontario, on 4 October 1817.
[PAO.MS154]

**BRYAN, MARY**, from Waterford on the St George of
London, to Maryland in 1677.
[SPDom#19/393][MSA.LO.Patents#15/553]

**BRYAN, PATRICK**, from Waterford on the St George of
London, to Maryland in 1677.
[SPDom#19/393][MSA.LO.Patents#15/553]

**BUCKLEY, JOHN**, born 1722, a coach-maker and
indentured servant who absconded from Thomas
Harvey, Garrison Ridge, Baltimore County, Maryland,
on 13 June 1756. [MdGaz.#582]

**BUCKLEY, MAURICE**, born 1788, from Fermoy, County
Cork, on the Stakesby to Quebec on 8 July 1823,
settled in Ramsay township, Ontario. [PAO.prp]

**BULLEN, THOMAS**, from Youghal to Maryland on the
Encrease of Youghal, master Philip Popplestone, in
1679. [Dorchester Co. Patents, WC#129]
[MSA.Patents#20/184]

**BURK, PATRICK**, late of the Royal Sappers, with his wife
and daughter, settled in Lanark, Ontario, 1 November
1820. [PAO.MS154]

**BURKE, DENIS, MD,** born 1752 in Ireland, late assistant
surgeon at West Point, died in Washington on 29 June
1852. [GM.NS38/433]

**BURKE, GEORGE R.**, from Ireland, settled in Marlborough,
Ontario, on 20 January 1822. [PAO.MS154]

**BURKE, HENRY**, from Ireland, settled in Marlborough,
Ontario, on 12 August 1822. [PAO.MS154]

**BURKE, JAMES,** from Ireland, settled in Marlborough,
Ontario, on 20 January 1822. [PAO.MS154]

**BURKE, JOHN**, from Waterford on the St George of London,
to Maryland in 1677.
[SPDom#19/393][MSA.LO.Patents#15/553]

**BURKE, MICHAEL,** from Ireland, settled in Huntley, Ontario,
on 20 September 1822. [PAO.MS154]

**BURLING, SAMUEL,** emigrated via Portrush on 27 August
1768 on the Providence, master Thomas Clark, bound
for New York, shipwrecked on 8 September.
[BNL#3283; 3.2.1769]

**BURN, MATTHEW,** a farmer from Ireland, settled in Smith, Newcastle, Ontario, on 15 April 1819. [PAO.MS154]

**BURN, MICHAEL,** a farmer from Ireland, settled in Smith, Newcastle, Ontario, on 15 April 1819. [PAO.MS154]

**BURN, PHILIP,** born 1702, dark complexion, an Irish indentured servant who absconded from King William County, Virginia, during 1752. [VaGaz.18.6.1752]

**BURNETT, JOSEPH,** a yeoman from Ireland, settled in Cavan, Newcastle, Ontario, on 19 September 1818. [PAO.MS154]

**BURNS, JOHN,** from Ireland, died in Buncombe County, North Carolina, in February 1830. [North Carolina Spectator; 14.5.1830]

**BURNS, THOMAS,** from Killileagh, County Down, settled as a farmer in Lower Providence, Chester County, Pennsylvania, Loyalist in 1776, returned to Ireland. [PRO.AO12.43.322]

**BURNS, THOMAS,** a former private of the 4th Royal Veteran Battalion, from Ireland, settled in Burgess, Ontario, on 30 June 1817. [PAO.MS154]

**BURNSIDE, JOHN,** from Ireland, settled in Cavan, Newcastle, Ontario, on 8 June 1818. [PAO.MS154]

**BURROWS, GEORGE,** from Ireland, settled in Huntley, Ontario, on 20 August 1821. [PAO.MS154]

**BURROWS, JOHN,** from Ireland, settled in Huntley, Ontario, on 10 August 1821. [PAO.MS154]

**BURROWS, WILLIAM,** from Ireland, late a private soldier of the 77th Regiment, with his wife and September 1822. [PAO.MS154]

**BUTLER, EDMUND,** born 1731, from Cork, 4 feet 6 inches tall, fair complexion, an indentured servant who absconded from Benjamin Catton in York Town, Virginia, on 17 February 1746. [VaGaz.20.3.1746]

**BUTLER, JANE,** from Waterford on the St George of London, to Maryland in 1677. [SPDom#19/393][MSA.LO.Patents#15/553]

**BUTLER, JOHN,** from Waterford on the St George of London, to Maryland in 1677. [SPDom#19/393][MSA.LO.Patents#15/553]

**BUTLER, JOHN,** (2) from Waterford on the <u>St George of London</u>, to Maryland in 1677.
[SPDom#19/393][MSA.LO.Patents#15/553]

**BUTLER, THOMAS,** born 1718, plasterer and indentured servant, absconded from Christopher Lowndes in Bladenburg on 6 August 1748; arrived in America 1747, a convict indentured servant, a carter or bricklayer/plasterer, absconded from Christopher Lowndes in Bladenburg, 1750(?). [MdGaz#177/282]

**BUTLER, TOBY,** from Waterford on the <u>St George of London</u>, to Maryland in 1677.
[SPDom#19/393][MSA.LO.Patents#15/553]

**BUTTER, WILLIAM,** born in Ireland, 5 feet 9 inches tall, swarthy complexion, a convict-indentured servant who absconded from Richard Graham in Dumfries, Virginia, in April 1759. [MdGaz#733]

**BYAM, ANTONY,** with his wife and son, from Ireland, settled in Lanark, Ontario, on 14 October 1821. [PAO.MS154]

**BYRNE, VALENTINE,** from Ireland, settled in Cavan, Newcastle, Ontario, on 20 April 1818. [PAO.MS154]

**BYRNE, WILLIAM,** a bookseller, son of Patrick Byrne a bookseller in Dublin, died in Philadelphia on 21 December 1805. [GM.76/182]

**CADDY, Mrs SARAH,** a widow from Ireland, settled in March, Ontario, on 23 August 1820. [PAO.MS154]

**CAGAN, BRIAN,** born 1689, an indentured servant and baker who absconded from Richard Barnes in Richmond County, Virginia, on 10 May 1738. [VaGaz.2.6.1738]

**CAHANE, PATRICK,** from Youghal to Maryland on the <u>Encrease of Youghal</u>, master Philip Popplestone, in 1679. [Dorchester Co. Patents, WC#129] [MSA.Patents#20/184]

**CAHILL, MICHAEL,** from Ireland, a former private of the 19th Dragoons, with his wife, son and daughter, settled in Drummond, Ontario, on 22 August 1817. [PAO.MS154]

**CAHILL, MCHAEL,** from Ireland, settled in Huntley, Ontario, on 31 July 1822. [PAO.MS154]

**CAHILL, THOMAS,** formerly a private of the Glengarry Fencibles, from Ireland, settled in Bathurst, Ontario, on 6 November 1816. [PAO.MS154]

**CAIN, MICHAEL,** an indentured servant who emigrated from Limerick to America on the Industry of Westhaven, master James Lowes, in March 1774. [Hook pp, DU]

**CALDWELL, JAMES,** from Ireland, settled in Huntley, Ontario, on 30 October1822. [PAO.MS154]

**CAMBIE, JEANNIE MAJOR,** third daughter of Charles Cambie from Castleton, Tipperaray, married John Hamilton, Tyrella House, Montreal, and of Hawkesbury, Ontario, in Ottawa on 3 June 1873. [EC#27685]

**CAMERON, JAMES,** a weaver from Ireland, settled in Toronto, Home, Ontario, on 15 August 1819. [PAO.MS154]

**CAMERON, SIMON,** born 1740, emigrated from Belfast on the Chichester, William Reed, to South Carolina, arrived in January 1768. [SCCJ.IV.1]

**CAMPBELL, ALEXANDER CALLENDER,** born 1842, son of William Campbell, Ballynaguid House, Londonderry, died at Hyde Park, Chicago, on 9 February 1878. [S#10,788]

**CAMPBELL, EDWARD,** married Miss Jones from Jamaica, in Grenada during 1800. [WHM#October, 1800/255]

**CAMPBELL, HUGH,** emigrated from Londonderry to New York on the Phoenix in 1818. [UF.35.18-41]

**CAMPBELL, JOHN,** an Irish indentured servant who absconded from John Mitchell in Urbanna, Virginia, during March 1739. [VaGaz.16.3.1739]

**CAMPBELL, JOHN,** emigrated via Portrush on 27 August 1768 on the Providence, master Thomas Clark, bound for New York, shipwrecked on 8 September. [BNL#3283; 3.2.1769]

**CAMPBELL, Mrs,** from Antrim, emigrated via Portrush on 27 August 1768 on the Providence, master Thomas Clark, shipwrecked on 8 September but rescued on 19 September by the Friendship of Bo'ness, master James Cowan, bound from Scotland to Charleston, South Carolina. [BNL#3283; 3.2.1769]

**CAMPBELL, MARY CALLENDAR,** third daughter of William Campbell, Ballynagard House, Londonderry, and wife of Joseph Thompson, died at Cottage Grove, Chicago, on 2 June 1880. [S#11,510]

**CAMPBELL, NEIL,** a laborer from Ireland, settled in Smith, Newcastle, Ontario, on 23 December 1818. [PAO.MS154]

**CAMPBELL, PATRICK,** from Ireland, settled in Goulburn, Ontario, on 29 September 1820. [PAO.MS154]

**CAMPBELL, WILLIAM,** from Ireland, settled in Goulburn, Ontario, on 31 October 1820. [PAO.MS154]

**CAMPBELL, .....,** from Londonderry, emigrated from the Clyde on the <u>Chipewa</u>, Captain Miller, bound for Montreal on 30 March 1840, wrecked off Cape Rozier on 30 April 1840. [EEC#20063]

**CANN, CATE,** from Waterford on the <u>St George of London</u>, to Maryland in 1677. [SPDom#19/393][MSA.LO.Patents#15/553]

**CANTWELL, ANN,** from Waterford on the <u>St George of London</u>, to Maryland in 1677. [SPDom#19/393][MSA.LO.Patents#15/553]

**CARBERRY, JAMES,** from Ireland, settled in Lanark, Ontario, on 5 September 1821. [PAO.MS154]

**CARDIFFE, RICHARD,** from Ireland, settled in Lanark, Ontario, on 5 September 1821. [PAO.MS154]

**CARELTON, THOMAS,** Ballincarrick, County Wicklow, purchased land in West New Jersey in 1664. [NYGBR#30]

**CAREW, JAMES,** from Waterford on the <u>St George of London</u>, to Maryland in 1677. [SPDom#19/393][MSA.LO.Patents#15/553]

**CAREY, FLORENCE,** born 1798, from Balhooley, County Cork, emigrated from Cove on the <u>Stakesby</u> to Quebec 8 July 1823, settled in Ramsay township, Ontario. [PAO.prp]

**CAREY, JOHN,** emigrated from the Cove of Cork on the <u>Hebe</u> bound for Quebec on 8 July 1823, settled in Ontario. [PRO.prp]

**CAREY, PETER,** an indentured servant who absconded from George Cooke, Leonard Town, Calvert County, Maryland, in August 1755. [MdGaz#537]

**CARNACHAN, MARY,** daughter of James Carnachan of Killyleagh {1777-1864} and Grace Carnachan {1780-1867}, settled in Norwich, America. [Killyleagh g/s, County Down]

15

**CARNEY, BATHOLEMEW,** born 1735, 5 feet 3 inches tall, an Irish indentured servant who absconded from Mark Kenton in Fauquier County, Virginia, on 16 September 1770. [VaGaz.11.10.1770]

**CARROLL, DAVID,** from Ireland, settled in Cavan, Newcastle, Ontario, on 13 September 1817. [PAO.MS154]

**CARROLL, JAMES,** from Waterford on the St George of London, to Maryland in 1677. [SPDom#19/393][MSA.LO.Patents#15/553]

**CARROLL, PATRICK,** born in Ireland around 1717, a convict indentured servant who absconded from John Martin an attorney at law in King William County, Virginia, on 5 May 1745. [VaGaz.30.5.1745]

**CARRY, JOHN,** an Irish indentured servant and blacksmith, who absconded from William Aylett in Essex County, Virginia, on 17 March 1739. [VaGaz.30.3.1739]

**CARSON, HUGH,** born 1727, Margaret born 1723, Jane born 1746, Margaret born 1748, James born 1749, Janet born 1750, Mary born 1752, Elizabeth born 1755, William born 1758, Hugh born 1760, and James born 1763, arrived in South Carolina in January 1768 on the brigantine Chichester, master William Reid, from Belfast. [SCCJ.34.1]

**CARSON, LUKE,** son of Luke Carson of Drumreagh {1775-1838} and Jane Carson {1786-1838}, settled in Savanna, Georgia. [Kilcairn g/s]

**CARTEE, OWEN,** born 1728, a convict indentured servant, absconded from William Byus in Dorchester County, Maryland, on 29 May 1748. [MdGaz#164]

**CARTER, GEORGE,** from Ireland, settled in Goulburn, Ontario, on 30 August 1821. [PAO.MS154]

**CARTER, GEORGE,** from Ireland, settled in Huntley, Ontario, on 14 August 1822. [PAO.MS154]

**CARTER, JOSEPH,** from Ireland, settled in Toronto, Home, Ontario, on 22 April 1819. [PAO.MS154]

**CARTER, WILLIAM,** from Ireland, settled in Huntley, Ontario, on 12 August 1822. [PAO.MS154]

**CARTHY, OWEN,** a free person from Ireland, arrived in Barbados during 1654. [Minutes of the Council of Barbados, 6.12.1654]

**CARTY, DENNIS**, from Waterford on the <u>St George of London</u>, to Maryland in 1677.
[SPDom#19/393][MSA.LO.Patents#15/553]

**CARTY, JAMES**, from Waterford on the <u>St George of London</u>, to Maryland in 1677.
[SPDom#19/393][MSA.LO.Patents#15/553]

**CARTY, MARY,** an indentured servant who emigrated from Limerick to America on the <u>Industry of Westhaven</u>, master James Lowes, in March 1774. [Hook pp, DU]

**CARTY, OWEN**, from Waterford on the <u>St George of London</u>, to Maryland in 1677.
[SPDom#19/393][MSA.LO.Patents#15/553]

**CARWICK, CHRISTOPHER**, from Waterford on the <u>St George of London</u>, to Maryland in 1677.
[SPDom#19/393][MSA.LO.Patents#15/553]

**CASSIDY, PETER,** from Ireland, settled in Goulburn, Ontario, on 30 November 1823. [PAO.MS154]

**CATHCART, ALEXANDER,** from Ireland, settled in Brock, Ontario, on 9 May 1818. [PAO.MS154]

**CATHCART, CASTLETON,** from Ireland, settled in Goulburn, Ontario, on 6 September 1822.
[PAO.MS154]

**CAUSDAY, CHARLES**, an indentured servant who absconded from Charles Griffith near the Severn River, Maryland, on 25 August 1754. [MdGaz#486]

**CAVANAGH, CATE**, from Waterford on the <u>St George of London</u>, to Maryland in 1677.
[SPDom#19/393][MSA.LO.Patents#15/553]

**CAVANAGH, DENNIS,** from Ireland, settled in Huntley, Ontario, on 10 August 1821. [PAO.MS154]

**CAVANAGH, JOHN,** from Ireland, settled in Huntley, Ontario, on 29 October 1820. [PAO.MS154]

**CAVANAGH, MICHAEL**, a former sergeant of the 70th Regiment, with his wife, son and daughter, settled in Bathurst, Ontario, 10 July 1820. [PAO.MS154]

**CAVENAGH, MARY**, from Waterford on the <u>St George of London</u>, to Maryland in 1677.
[SPDom#19/393][MSA.LO.Patents#15/553]

**CENTERELL, GODFREY**, a yeoman, Queens County, Ireland, purchased land in West Jersey, 1664.
[NYGBR#30]

**CHALMERS, SAMUEL,** an indentured servant who emigrated from Belfast on the Bruerton of Liverpool, master John Fowler, to Philadelphia in 1729. [PRONI#D354/71]

**CHAMBERS, HANNAH,** an indentured servant who emigrated from Limerick to America on the Industry of Westhaven, master Jamews Lowes, in March 1774. [Hook pp, DU]

**CHAMBERS, RANDALL,** settled in Chester County, Pennsylvania, before 1724. [CCA. J.Davenport file]

**CHAPMAN, JOHN,** sr., with his wife, two sons and one daughter, from Ireland, settled in Lanark, Ontatio, on 1 June 1821. [PAO.MS154]

**CHAPMAN, JOHN,** jr., from Ireland, settled in Lanark, Ontatio, on 1 June 1821. [PAO.MS154]

**CHAPMAN, WILLIAM,** with his wife, from Ireland, settled in Ramsay, Ontario, on 14 April 1821. [PAO.MS154]

**CHAPPELL, Captain,** from Ireland, taken hostage on St Kitts by the Spanish in 1631. [Haylukt Society Publications, 2nd series, Vol.56, fo.13]

**CHARLETON, EDWARD,** a weaver and indentured servant, absconded from Henry Morgan in Baltimore County, Maryland, in June 1747. [MdGaz#112]

**CHEARNLEY, ANTHONY,** from Ireland, settled in Monaghan, Newcastle, Ontario, on 16 April 1818. [PAO.MS154]

**CHEARNLEY, EDWARD,** from Ireland, settled in Monaghan, Newcastle, Ontario, on 16 April 1818. [PAO.MS154]

**CHEARNLEY, JOSEPH,** from Ireland, settled in Monaghan, Newcastle, Ontario, on 16 April 1818. [PAO.MS154]

**CHEARNLEY, RICHARD,** from Ireland, settled in Monaghan, Newcastle, Ontario, on 16 April 1818. [PAO.MS154]

**CHEARNLEY, SAMUEL,** from Ireland, settled in Halliwell, Midland, Ontario, on 16 April 1818. [PAO.MS154]

**CHESNEY, ALEXANDER,** born in 1755, emigrated to South Carolina in 1772, a Loyalist, returned to Ireland, possibly died in 1821. [BM.Add.#32627]

**CHILD, OWEN,** from Waterford on the St George of London, to Maryland in 1677. [SPDom#19/393][MSA.LO.Patents#15/553]

**CHURCHILL, SAMUEL**, late of the Sappers and Miners, with his wife and three sons, land grant in Burgess, Ontario, on 18 September 1819. [PAO.MS154]

**CLAHAN, TIMOTHY**, with Margarette, Joanna and Catherine, from Churchtown, County Cork, emigrated from the Cove of Cork on the Hebe, bound for Quebec on 8 July 1823, settled in Pakenham, Ontario. [PAO.prp]

**CLARK, JOHN**, formerly a private of the Canadian Fencibles, with his wife, two sons and two daughters, from Ireland, settled in Burgess, Ontario, on 30 September 1816. [PAO.MS154]

**CLARKE, GEORGE**, from Ireland, settled in March, Ontario, on 23 August 1820. [PAO.MS154]

**CLARKE, WILLIAM**, from Ireland, a former sergeant of the Carlow Militia, with his wife, four sons and two daughters, settled in Drummond, Ontario, on 12 August 1817 and in Montague, Ontario, 30 November 1817. [PAO.MS154]

**CLARKEY, WILLIAM**, merchant, Dublin, purchased land in West New Jersey in 1664. [NYGBR#30]

**CLEARY, CONNOR**, an indentured servant who emigrated from Limerick to America on the Industry of Westhaven, master James Lowes, in March 1774. [Hook pp, DU]

**CLELAND, JOSEPH**, with his wife Margaret, and infant son James, emigrated from Belfast via Liverpool to New York in May 1853, settled in Royalton, Lockport, New York, and by 1857 had moved to East Guillymsburg, Canada. [Ulster Folklife#3/64]

**CLYNTON, THOMAS**, from Waterford on the St George of London, to Maryland in 1677. [SPDom#19/393][MSA.LO.Patents#15/553]

**COCHRAN, WILLIAM**, from Waterford on the St George of London, to Maryland in 1677. [SPDom#19/393][MSA.LO.Patents#15/553]

**COCHRANE, JOSEPH**, settled in Chester County, Pennsylvania, before 1722. [CCA.inv#285]

**COCKBURN, ANN**, from Waterford on the St George of London, to Maryland in 1677. [SPDom#19/393][MSA.LO.Patents#15/553]

**COCKBURN, JOHN,** from Ireland, settled in Huntley, Ontario, on 16 March 1822. [PAO.MS154]

**CODD, ABRAHAM,** with his wife, son and daughter, settled in Drummond, Ontario, 10 March 1820. [PAO.MS154]

**COFFE, JAMES,** an indentured servant who emigrated from Belfast on the Bruerton of Liverpool, master John Fowler, to Philadelphia in 1729. [PRONI#D354/71]

**COLE, JOHN,** from Louth, Ireland, settled in Westminster, London, Ontario, on 19 March 1818. [PAO.MS154]

**COLEMAN, ANTHONY,** from Waterford on the St George of London, to Maryland in 1677. [SPDom#19/393][MSA.LO.Patents#15/553]

**COLEMAN, DANIEL,** late of the Royal Sappers, with his wife and three sons, settled in Lanark, Ontario, on 1 November 1820. [PAO.MS154]

**COLEMAN, JOHN,** alias John Nabb, an Irish indentured servant and convict who arrived in Virginia on the Forward galley in 1737, and absconded from John Rolls in Caroline County, Virginia, on 27 August 1738. [VaGaz.22.9.1738]

**COLEMAN, THOMAS,** from Waterford on the St George of London, to Maryland in 1677. [SPDom#19/393][MSA.LO.Patents#15/553]

**COLLINS, JOHN,** alias John Butler, an Irish indentured servant who absconded from Matthew Maves in Prince George County, Virginia, on 14 November 1739. [VaGaz.30.11.1739]

**COLLINS, JOHN,** born in Ireland 1821, a merchant, settled in Anderson County, Texas, by 1850. [C]

**COLLINS, THOMAS,** from Ireland, settled in Beckwith, Ontario, on 1 May 1820. [PAO.MS154]

**COLLINS, TIMOTHY,** a merchant from the Isle of Speike, County Cork, was killed by a Dutch privateer when returning from the West Indies in 1666, his widow Katherine petitioned the King in July 1666. [SPDom#1666/577]

**COLLONEY, RICHARD,** 5 feet 10 inches, an Irish indentured servant who absconded from Robert Rennolds in Port Royal, Caroline County, Virginia, on 28 August 1774. [VaGaz.29.9.1774]

**CONDON, JOHN**, from Youghal to Maryland on the
Encrease of Youghal, master Philip Popplestone, in
1679. [Dorchester Co. Patents, WC#129]
[MSA.Patents#20/184]

**CONDON, RICHARD,** an Irish shoemaker, deserted from
Benjamin Stoddart's Company of militia in Annapolis,
August 1746. [MdGaz#68]

**CONLIN, FRANCIS,** with his wife and three daughters, from
Ireland, settled in Ramsay, Ontario, on 10 May 1821.
[PAO.MS154]

**CONN, JOHN,** from Ireland, settled in Lanark, Ontario, on 5
September 1821. [PAO.MS154]

**CONNELL, KITTY,** an indentured servant who emigrated
from Limerick to America on the Industry of
Westhaven, master Jamews Lowes, in March 1774.
[Hook pp, DU]

**CONNELL, or SULLIVANE, MARGARET,** born in Ireland
around 1710, a convict indentured servant who
absconded from Richard Taylor, Petersburg, Virginia,
in 1755. [VaGaz.19.9.1755]

**CONNELL, MAURICE,** an indentured servant who emigrated
from Limerick to America on the Industry of
Westhaven, master James Lowes, in March 1774.
[Hook pp, DU]

**CONNELL, MORGAN,** from Youghal to Maryland on the
Encrease of Youghal, master Philip Popplestone, in
1679. [Dorchester Co. Patents, WC#129]
[MSA.Patents#20/184]

**CONNELL, PATRICK,** an indentured servant who emigrated
from Limerick to America on the Industry of
Westhaven, master James Lowes, in March 1774.
[Hook pp, DU]

**CONNELLY, MARGARET,** an indentured servant who
emigrated from Limerick to America on the Industry of
Westhaven, master James Lowes, in March 1774.
[Hook pp, DU]

**CONNOR, EDMUND,** an Irish indentured servant and
blacksmith, absconded from Charles Ridgeley,
Patapsco Ferry, Baltimore County, Maryland, in June
1746. [MdGaz#59]

**CONNOR, HONOR,** from Waterford on the St George of London, to Maryland in 1677.
[SPDom#19/393][MSA.LO.Patents#15/553]

**CONNOR, MARTIN**, from Ireland, formerly in the Royal Navy, with wife and daughter, settled in Drummond, Ontario, 6 April 1818. [PAO.MS154]

**CONNOR, MICHAEL,** an indentured servant who emigrated from Limerick to America on the Industry of Westhaven, master James Lowes, in March 1774.
[Hook pp, DU]

**CONNOR, MICHAEL,** from Ireland, a former privateof the Carlow Militia, with his wife, four sons and one daughter, settled in Oxford, Ontario, on 9 July 1817.
[PAO.MS154]

**CONNOR, ROGER,** an Irish indentured servant, absconded from William Cumming in Gilpin's Plantation, near the head of the Patuxent River, Maryland, on 2 December 1746. [MdGaz#92]

**CONNOR, THOMAS**, late of the York Chasseurs, with his wife, son and daughter, land grant in Bathurst, Ontario, 22 September 1819. [PAO.MS154]

**CONNOR, TIMOTHY,** from Youghal to Maryland on the Encrease of Youghal, master Philip Popplestone, in 1679. [Dorchester Co. Patents, WC#129]
[MSA.Patents#20/184]

**CONNORS, JAMES,** an indentured servant who emigrated from Limerick to America on the Industry of Westhaven, master James Lowes, in March 1774.
[Hook pp, DU]

**CONWAY, JOHN,** an indentured servant who emigrated from Limerick to America on the Industry of Westhaven, master James Lowes, in March 1774.
[Hook pp, DU]

**COOK, JOHN,** from Ireland, settled in March, Ontario, on 23 August 1820. [PAO.MS154]

**COPELAND, RICHARD,** from Ireland, settled in Beckwith, Ontario, on 29 November 1821. [PAO.MS154]

**CORBAN, MARGARET**, from Waterford on the St George of London, to Maryland in 1677.
[SPDom#19/393][MSA.LO.Patents#15/553]

**CORKERY, MICHAEL,** born 1784, with Ellen born 1803, Elisa born 1805, Pat born 1807, Bridget born 1813, Mary born 1820 and Michael born 1820, emigrated from Cove on the Stakesby to Quebec on 8 July 1823, settled in Ramsay township, Ontario. [PAO.prp]

**CORNAN, JAMES,** a former private of the 104th Regiment, from Ireland, settled in Beckwith, Ontario, on 6 June 1817. [PAO.MS154]

**CORNELIUS, PATRICK,** an Irish indentured servant, made a freeman in Barbados in December 1656. [Minutes of the Council of Barbados, 12.1656]

**COROHAN, MARY,** from Youghal to Maryland on the Encrease of Youghal, master Philip Popplestone, in 1679. [Dorchester Co. Patents, WC#129] [MSA.Patents#20/184]

**CORRANE, MARGARET,** from Youghal to Maryland on the Encrease of Youghal, master Philip Popplestone, in 1679. [Dorchester Co. Patents, WC#129] [MSA.Patents#20/184]

**CORRELL, THOMAS,** an indentured servant who emigrated from Belfast on the Bruerton of Liverpool, master John Fowler, to Philadelphia in 1729. [PRONI#D354/71]

**CORREY, ROBERT,** possibly from County Down, settled in South Carolina before 1776, a Loyalist, later in Georgia and East Florida, died in England during 1786. [PRO.AO12.102.27]

**COSTELLO, MATTHEW,** from Ireland, settled in Goulburn, Ontario, on 30 October 1822. [PAO.MS154]

**COSTICAN, CATE,** from Waterford on the St George of London, to Maryland in 1677. [SPDom#19/393][MSA.LO.Patents#15/553]

**COSTICAN, DENIS,** from Waterford on the St George of London, to Maryland in 1677. [SPDom#19/393][MSA.LO.Patents#15/553]

**COUGHIN, HUGH,** from Ireland, settled in Beck, Ontario, on 30 November 1821. [PAO.MS154]

**COUGHLIN, HONOR,** from Waterford on the St George of London, to Maryland in 1677. [SPDom#19/393][MSA.LO.Patents#15/553]

**COUGHLIN, JOHN,** from Youghal to Maryland on the Encrease of Youghal, master Philip Popplestone, in

1679. [Dorchester Co. Patents, WC#129]
[MSA.Patents#20/184]

**COULTER, ANDREW,** an indentured servant who emigrated
from Belfast on the Bruerton of Liverpool, master John
Fowler, to Philadelphia in 1729. [PRONI#D354/71]

**COURTNEY,JOSEPH,** from Ireland, formerly of the 5th
Dragoon Guards, with his wife, settled in Burgess,
Ontario, on 15 December 1817. [PAO.MS154]

**COVENY, PETER,** from Waterford on the St George of
London, to Maryland in 1677.
[SPDom#19/393][MSA.LO.Patents#15/553]

**COVERANE, JOHN,** from Youghal to Maryland on the
Encrease of Youghal, master Philip Popplestone, in
1679. [Dorchester Co. Patents, WC#129]
[MSA.Patents#20/184]

**COWEN, JAMES,** a Presbyterian minister from Belfast, who
settled in Goldsboro, North Carolina, former husband
of Sarah Cowan of Ballykees, County Down, 1844.
[NCSA.CR103.928.12]

**CRAFE, EDMOND,** from Waterford on the St George of
London, to Maryland in 1677.
[SPDom#19/393][MSA.LO.Patents#15/553]

**CRAFORD, ANN,** from Waterford on the St George of
London, to Maryland in 1677.
[SPDom#19/393][MSA.LO.Patents#15/553]

**CRAIG, WILLIAM,** born in County Antrim during 1799,
arrived in New York in January 1819, settled in Salem,
North Carolina, naturalised in Stokes County, North
Carolina, on 17 April 1821. [NCSA.CR090.3111/1]

**CRAIG, WILLIAM,** from Ireland, settled in Goulburn, Ontario,
on 30 November 1821. [PAO.MS154]

**CRAMPTON, CHARLES,** with his wife and son, arrived on
the Maria 1819, settled in Drummond, Ontario, 18
March 1820. [PAO.MS154]

**CRAMVILLE, WILLIAM,** from Ireland, settled in Ontario, on
3 August 1818. [PAO.MS154]

**CRANSBROUGH, NELL,** from Waterford on the St George
of London, to Maryland in 1677.
[SPDom#19/393][MSA.LO.Patents#15/553]

**CRAWFORD, GEORGE,** from Ireland, settled in Cavan,
Newcastle, Ontario, on 21 August 1818. [PAO.MS154]

CRAWFORD, ..., son of Daniel Crawford, probably in the parish of Billy, County Antrim, settled in Philadelphia by 1837. [PRONI#D1828/3]

CRONY, RICHARD, a former corporal of the York Chasseurs, settled in Drummond, Ontario, 8 July 1820. [PAO.MS154]

CROSBIE, THOMAS, a former sergeant of the 70th Regiment, with his wife and three daughters, land grant in Bathurst, Ontario, 2 September 1819. [PAO.MS154]

CROUGH,JAMES, from Waterford on the St George of London, to Maryland in 1677. [SPDom#19/393][MSA.LO.Patents#15/553]

CROZIER, JOHN, , a yeoman from Ireland, settled in Cavan Newcastle, Ontario, on 12 September 1818. [PAO.MS154]

CRUMP, HENRY, formerly a private of the 90th Regiment, from Ireland, settled in Burgess, Ontario, on 18 September 1816. [PAO.MS154]

CRUMP, JOHN, formerly a private of the 90th Regiment, from Ireland, settled in Burgess, Ontario, on 18 September 1816. [PAO.MS154]

CUDDY, WILLIAM, born 1707 in Ireland, an indentured servant who absconded from John Shortwell in Orange County, Virginia, on 19 July 1745. [VaGaz.19.9.1745]

CULLEN, EDWARD, an Irish indentured servant who absconded from Thomas Thorp in Essex County, Virginia, on 2 December 1738. [VaGaz.8.12.1738]

CULLEN, JAMES, from Ireland, settled in Goulburn, Ontario, on 3 March 1822. [PAO.MS154]

CULLEN, MICHAEL, formerly a private of the 8th [King's] Regiment, from Ireland, settled in Burgess, Ontario, on 30 September 1816. [PAO.MS154]

CUMMINGS, FRANCIS H., from Ireland, a former Lieutenant of the 104th Regiment, settled in Oxford, Burgess, Ontario, on 31 July 1817. [PAO.MS154]

CUMMINGS, MARTIN, born in Mayo on 21 December 1867, fair complexion, 5'7", 130 lb, brown hair, blue eyes, emigrated via Queenstown, Ireland, to New York on the Gallia 10 July 1886, roadmaster for the railroad, naturalised on 22 August 1910 in Oklahoma City. [Oklahoma Courthouse Naturalisation book#3/162]

**CUNNINGHAM,JAMES,** a joiner, emigrated in 1752, an indentured servant who absconded from Robert Evans, near the head of Elk River, Cecil County, Maryland, on 24 February 1753. [MdGaz#409]

**CUNNINGHAM, JAMES,** with his wife and son, from Ireland, settled in Lanark, Ontario, on 8 September 1817. [PAO.MS154]

**CUNNINGHAM, JOHN,** emigrated from Belfast on 27 September 1795 on board the America bound for Boston, arrived there on 12 December 1795. [PRONI#D394/2]

**CUNNINGHAM, SAMUEL,** jr., in St Vincent and in Martinique 1792 to 1796. [PRONI#DOD.1108/3-11]

**CURRY, JOHN,** a whisky distiller from County Antrim, settled in Lancaster County, Pennsylvania, in 1773, Loyalist, returned to Ireland. [PRO.AO12.42.86]

**CURTIN, WILLIAM,** an indentured servant who emigrated from Limerick to America on the Industry of Westhaven, master James Lowes, in March 1774. [Hook pp, DU]

**CUSACK, PATRICK,** from Ireland, settled in Goulburn, Ontario, on 20 January 1821. [PAO.MS154]

**CUSICK, ANNIVER,** born 1794, from Charleville, County Cork, emigrated from Cove on the Stakesby to Quebec on 8 July 1823, settled in Pakenham, Ontario. [PAO.prp]

**CUSLAN, JOHN,** from Ireland, settled in Lanark, Ontario, on 5 September 1821. [PAO.MS154]

**DAHILL, TIMOTHY,** from Newmarket, County Limerick, emigrated from the Cove of Cork on the Hebe bound for Quebec on 8 July 1823, settled in Ramsay, Ontario. [PAO.prp]

**DAILY, JAMES,** from Ireland, late of the Royal Sappers, settled in Lanark, Ontario, on 1 November 1820. [PAO]

**DALEY, HUGH,** formerly a sergeant of the 8th [King's] Regiment, with his wife, son and daughter, from Ireland, settled in Burgess, Ontario, on 20 September 1816. [PAO.MS154]

**DALEY, JAMES,** jr., from Ireland, settled in Huntley, Ontario, on 26 January 1821. [PAO.MS154]

**DALEY, ROBERT,** from Ireland, settled in Huntley, Ontario, on 26 January 1821. [PAO.MS154]

**DALTON, ELLEN,** from Waterford on the St George of London, to Maryland in 1677. [SPDom#19/393][MSA.LO.Patents#15/553]

**DALY, HUGH,** from Ireland, a former sergeant major, settled in Leeds, Ontario, 30 November 1817. [PAO.MS154]

**DALY, LAUGHLIN,** from Waterford on the St George of London, to Maryland in 1677. [SPDom#19/393][MSA.LO.Patents#15/553]

**DALZIEL, ALEXANDER,** from Ireland, settled in Cavan, Newcastle, Ontario, on 24 September 1817. [PAO.MS154]

**DANCY, THOMAS,** with his wife and son, from Ireland, settled in Dalhousie, Ontario, on 10 May 1822. [PAO.MS154]

**DANIEL, EDMOND,** (1), from Waterford on the St George of London, to Maryland in 1677. [SPDom#19/393][MSA.LO.Patents#15/553]

**DANIEL, EDMOND,** (2), from Waterford on the St George of London, to Maryland in 1677. [SPDom#19/393][MSA.LO.Patents#15/553]

**DANNISSON, GEORGE,** an indentured servant who absconded from Kent Island, Maryland, in July 1750. [MdGaz#273]

**DANSCOMB or DUNGAN, PATRICK,** an indentured servant who absconded from Zachariah Mackubin in Baltimore County, Maryland, on 10 March 1748. [MdGaz#208]

**DAVIS, DANIEL,** from Ireland, settled in Cavan, Newcastle, Ontario, on 20 July 1818. [PAO.MS154]

**DAVIS, HUGH,** from Ireland, settled in Cavan, Newcastle, Ontario, on 2 September 1818. [PAO.MS154]

**DAWSON, JOHN,** a yeoman from Ireland, settled in Cavan Newcastle, Ontario, on 7 November 1818. [PAO.MS154]

**DAY, MARGARET,** from Waterford on the St George of London, to Maryland in 1677. [SPDom#19/393][MSA.LO.Patents#15/553]

**DAYLEY, HANNAH,** an Irish tinker and convict indentured servant who absconded from William Taite in

Northumberland County, Virginia, in March 1767.
[VaGaz.26.3.1767]

**DAYLEY, WILLIAM,** an Irish tinker and convict indentured servant who absconded from William Taite in Northumberland County, Virginia, in March 1767. [VaGaz.26.3.1767]

**DEACON, HENRY,** from Ireland, settled in Ramsay, Ontario, on 9 April 1821. [PAO.MS154]

**DEAN, HUGH,** born 1730, an Irish indentured servant who absconded from Thomas Dansie in King William County, Virginia, during 1751. [VaGaz.4.7.1751]

**DE COURCEY, JAMES,** a yeoman from Ireland, settled in Smith, Newcastle, Ontario, on 19 January 1819. [PAO.MS154]

**DELANY, JOHN,** from Waterford on the St George of London, to Maryland in 1677.
[SPDom#19/393][MSA.LO.Patents#15/553]

**DELANY, MICHAEL,** from Waterford on the St George of London, to Maryland in 1677.
[SPDom#19/393][MSA.LO.Patents#15/553]

**DELANY, MICHAEL,** from Ireland, settled in Cavan, Newcastle, Ontario, on 2 May 1818. [PAO.MS154]

**DELEUREY, JOHN,** born 1799, with Biddy born 1803, from Mallow, County Cork, emigrated from Cove on the Stakesby to Quebec on 8 July 1823, settled in Ramsay township, Ontario. [PAO.prp]

**DEMPSEY, EDWARD,** born 1728, a barber and indentured servant who absconded from Thomas Chittam in Bladensburg in June 1754. [MdGaz#477]

**DEMPSEY, JOHN,** a farmer from Ireland, settled in Smith, Newcastle, Ontario, on 15 April 1819. [PAO.MS154]

**DENNIS, JOHN,** joiner, Cork, purchased land in West New Jersey in 1664. [NYGBR#30]

**DENNIS, ROWLAND,** a joiner and indentured servant who absconded from Rowland Carnan, Elk Ridge Landing, Maryland, in July 1753. [MdGaz#426]

**DENNIS, SAMUEL,** merchant, Cork, purchased land in West New Jersey in 1664. [NYGBR#30]

**DENNISE, ELIZABETH,** born 1692, arrived in South Carolina in January 1768 on the brigantine Chichester, master William Reid, from Belfast. [SCCJ.34.1]

**DENNISON, JOHN,** a weaver, possibly from County Down, settled in Franklin, Pennsylvania, by 1789. [PRONI#T2294/1]

**DENNISON, WILLIAM,** from Ireland, landed from the Belvoir on 17 August 1817, settled in Elmsley, Ontario, on 30 September 1817. [PAO]

**DEVLIN, CHARLES,** settled in Drummond, Ontario, 17 April 1820. [PAO.MS154]

**DEVLIN, MICHAEL,** settled in Drummond, Ontario, 17 April 1820. [PAO.MS154]

**DEYELL, JAMES,** a yeoman from Ireland, settled in Cavan, Newcastle, Ontario, on 9 August 1818. [PAO.MS154]

**DEYERMAND, JOHN,** in Albany, New York, son of William Deyermand {1734-1784} and Agnes Deyermand {1745-1815}. [Drumbog g/s, County Down]

**DEYERMAND, WILLIAM,** in Albany, New York, son of William Deyermand {1734-1784} and Agnes Deyermand {1745-1815}. [Drumbog g/s, County Down]

**DICKEY, HECTOR,** born 1744, arrived in South Carolina in January 1768 on the brigantine Chichester, master William Reid, from Belfast. [SCCJ.34.1]

**DICKEY, JANE,** born 1709, arrived in South Carolina in January 1768 on the brigantine Chichester, master William Reid, from Belfast. [SCCJ.34.1]

**DICKEY, ROBERT,** born 1736, Susannah born 1734, William born 1760, James born 1761, Elizabeth born 1763, and Jane born 1764, arrived in South Carolina in January 1768 on the brigantine Chichester, master William Reid, from Belfast. [SCCJ.34.1]

**DICKSON, ROBERT,** a yeoman from Tyrone, Ireland, settled in Thurlaw, Ontario, on 23 July 1817. [PAO.MS154]

**DICKSON, ROBERT,** with his wife, son and daughter, from Ireland, landed from the Saltham on 1 August 1817, settled in Yonge, Ontario, on 6 October 1817. [PAO.MS154]

**DICKSON, WILLIAM,** a mason from Ireland, settled in Smith, Newcastle, Ontario, on 23 December 1818. [PAO.MS154]

**DICKSON, WILLIAM JAMES,** born in Aughnocloy 20 February 1890, fair complexion, 5'8", 154 lb, brown hair, blue eyes, emigrated via Belfast to Quebec on the

Lake Manitoba 21 June 1909, a laborer, nat.6 February 1911 in Oklahoma City. [Oklahoma Courthouse Naturalisation book 3/191]

DILLON, DARBY, from Waterford on the St George of London, to Maryland in 1677. [SPDom#19/393][MSA.LO.Patents#15/553]

DILLON, JOHN BLAKE, a 'Young Irelander', settled in New York during 1849. [TCD.MS#6455]

DILWORTH, WILLIAM, from Ireland, settled in Marlborough, Ontario, on 30 October 1822. [PAO.MS154]

DIXON, GEORGE, born 1809, from Ballybay, County Monaghan, died in St John, New Brunswick, 10 June 1872. [S#9028]

DIXON, JOHN, born in Ireland 1736, 5 feet 2 inches tall, an indentured servant and smith who absconded from John Hobdy in Gloucester County, Virginia, in September 1755. [VaGaz.10.10.1755]

DOBSON, JOHN, from Ireland, settled in Ramsay, Ontario, on 6 May 1821. [PAO.MS154]

DOBSON, JOSEPH, from Ireland, settled in Ramsay, Ontario, on 10 May 1822. [PAO.MS154]

DOCKERAL, BENJAMIN, with his wife, son and daughter, from Ireland, settled in Ramsay, Ontario, on 10 May 1821. [PAO.MS154]

DOHERTY, JOHN, with Jude, Pat, Edward and Daniel, from Churchtown, County Cork, emigrated from the Cove of Cork on the Hebe bound for Quebec on 8 July 1823, settled in Pakenham, Ontario. [PAO.MS154]

DOIEL, PHILIP, an indentured servant who absconded from John and Enoch Bailey, Baltimore County, Maryland, on 13 July 1755. [MdGaz#532]

DOLAN, BRIDGET, 5 feet 6 inches tall, with a fresh complexion, an Irish indentured servant who absconded from Joseph Gilliam in Williamsburg, Virginia, on 19 July 1746. [VaGaz.24.7.1746]

DOLAN, MORRIS, from Youghal to Maryland on the Encrease of Youghal, master Philip Popplestone, in 1679. [Dorchester Co. Patents, WC#129] [MSA.Patents#20/184]

**DOLAN, ROGER**, from Waterford on the St George of London, to Maryland in 1677.
[SPDom#19/393][MSA.LO.Patents#15/553]

**DOLLASON, ROBERT,** an indentured servant who absconded from Thomas Daviss, near Snowden's Ironworks, Maryland, on 1 September 1754.
[MdGaz#487]

**DOLLY, DAVID**, from Youghal to Maryland on the Encrease of Youghal, master Philip Popplestone, in 1679.
[Dorchester Co. Patents, WC#129]
[MSA.Patents#20/184]

**DONAGH, DERBY,** from Waterford on the St George of London, to Maryland in 1677.
[SPDom#19/393][MSA.LO.Patents#15/553]

**DONAGHUE, PATRICK,** born 1779, wife Anne born 1783, children Katherine born 1816, Margaret born 1819, and Mary born 1821, from Mallow, County Cork, emigrated from Cove on the Stakesby bound for Quebec on 8 July 1823, settled in Ramsay township, Ontario.
[PAO.MS154]

**DONAHOE, PATRICK,** 5 feet 7 inches tall, an Irish indentured servant who absconded from Jacob Andrew Minitree in Charles County, Maryland, on 2 April 1751.
[VaGaz.7.3.1751]

**DONAHUE, MICHAEL,** from Ireland, settled in Goulburn, Ontario, on 30 July 1821. [PAO.MS154]

**DONALDSON, JOHN,** from Ireland, settled in Cavan, Newcastle, Ontario, on 20 July 1818. [PAO.MS154]

**DONALLY, HENRY,** born 1719, an Irish indentured servant who absconded from Mary Bordland in Hampton, Virginia, on 28 November 1736. [VaGaz.3.12.1736]

**DONALSON, HUGH,** born 1739, and Mary born 1744, arrived in South Carolina in January 1768 on the brigantine Chichester, master William Reid, from Belfast. [SCCJ.34.1]

**DORINGTON, HUGH,** from Ireland, settled in Huntley, Ontario, on 2 July 1821. [PAO.MS154]

**DORINGTON, JAMES,** from Ireland, settled in Huntley, Ontario, on 2 July 1821. [PAO.MS154]

**DORMEDY, MICHAEL**, from Waterford on the St George of London, to Maryland in 1677.
[SPDom#19/393][MSA.LO.Patents#15/553]

**DOTEN, JOHN,** an Irish indentured servant and maltster/brewer who absconded from Daniel Horby in Richmond County, Virginia, on 3 September 1737.
[VaGen.14.10.1737]

**DOUBIN, MARGARET**, from Waterford on the St George of London, to Maryland in 1677.
[SPDom#19/393][MSA.LO.Patents#15/553]

**DOUGAN, PRISCELLA**, from Waterford on the St George of London, to Maryland in 1677.
[SPDom#19/393][MSA.LO.Patents#15/553]

**DOUGHERTY, ARTHUR,** from Ireland, settled in Drummond, Ontario, on 4 October 1821. [PAO.MS154]

**DOUGHERTY, DANIEL,** emigrated via Portrush on 27 August 1768 on the Providence, master Thomas Clark, bound for New York, shipwrecked on 8 September 1768. [BNL#3283, 3.2.1769]

**DOUGHERTY, JAMES**, from Ireland, formerly of the 4th Veterans, settled in Drummond, Ontario, on 16 March 1818. [PAO.MS154]

**DOUGHERTY, JAMES,** with his wife and five daughters, from Ireland, settled in Ramsay, Ontario, on 24 August 1822. [PAO.MS154]

**DOWLING, JAMES,** born 1725, an Irish indentured servant, absconded from Stourton Edwards, St Mary's County, Maryland, on 4 October 1745. [MdGaz#26]

**DOWNING, ANDREW,** from Ireland, settled in Goulburn, Ontario, on 25 October 1822. [PAO.MS154]

**DOYLE, JOHN,** from Ireland, settled in Cavan, Newcastle, Ontario, on 15 December 1817. [PAO.MS154]

**DOYLE, JONATHAN,** from Ireland, settled in Cavan, Newcastle, Ontario, on 15 December 1817.
[PAO.MS154]

**DOYLE, PATRICK,** from Ireland, landed from the Eolus in 1820, settled in Drummond, Ontario, on 30 March 1821. [PAO.MS154]

**DRAKE, WILLIAM,** born 1800, from Kildorrey, County Cork, emigrated from Cove on the Stakesby to Quebec on 8

July 1823, settled in Ramsay township, Ontario.
[PAO.prp]

**DRISCOLL, CORNEL,** from Youghal to Maryland on the
Encrease of Youghal, master Philip Popplestone, in
1679. [Dorchester Co. Patents, WC#129]
[MSA.Patents#20/184]

**DRISCOLL, MICHAEL,** born in Ireland during 1742,
emigrated from Dublin to America on the Burwell,
Captain Huison, in 1756, an indentured servant who
absconded from the Carlisle a ship in the James River,
Virginia, in August 1756. [VaGaz.3.9.1756]

**DRUM, BRYON,** 5 feet 7 inches tall, an Irish indentured
servant who absconded from Philip Cassay in
Frederick County, Maryland, in January 1775.
[VaGaz.18.2.1775]

**DUDGEON, THOMAS,** landed from the Argo in September
1820, settled in Bathurst, Ontario, on 17 March 1821.
[PAO.MS154]

**DUFF, JAMES,** son of John Duff in Coagh, County Tyrone,
settled in Philadelphia by 1819. [PRONI.t3102/1/12]

**DUFFY, CHARLES,** from Ireland, settled in Westminster,
London, Ontario, on 15 December 1817. [PAO.MS154]

**DUFFY, JOHN,** from Ireland, settled in Cavan, Newcastle,
Ontario, on 15 December 1817. [PAO.MS154]

**DULMAGE, GARRET,** with Sarah, Margaret, Richard and
Lawrence, emigrated from the Cove of Cork on the
Hebe bound for Quebec on 8 July 1823, settled in
Ramsay, Ontario. [PAO.prp]

**DUNBAR, JOHN,** a former corporal of the 4th Royal Veteran
Battalion, with his wife, two sons and two daughters,
from Ireland, settled in Bathurst, Ontario, on 30 June
1817. [PAO.MS154]

**DUNCAN, MARGARET,** possibly from County Tyrone,
settled in Philadelphia by 1774. [PRONI#D1140/2]

**DUNCOMBE, DANIEL,** an Irish indentured servant in
Barbados, 1656. [Minutes of the Council of Barbados,
12.1656]

**DUNFIELD, JAMES,** from Ireland, settled in Goulburn,
Ontario, on 4 September 1822. [PAO.MS154]

**DUNLAP, JOHN,** born in Strabane, County Tyrone, during
1746, settled in Philadelphia by 1755, printer of the

*Pennsylvania Packet.* A militia captain. Died in 1812.
[PRONI#T1336/1/22]

**DUNN,** or **BLACK, PERCIE,** a vagrant imprisoned in
Dundalk, to be transported to the colonies in 1728.
[NLI#ms11949]

**DUNN, ROBERT,** from Waterford on the St George of
London, to Maryland in 1677.
[SPDom#19/393][MSA.LO.Patents#15/553]

**DUNN, WILLIAM,** from Waterford on the St George of
London, to Maryland in 1677.
[SPDom#19/393][MSA.LO.Patents#15/553]

**DUNNOHU, REAGE,** an Irish indentured servant of Edward
Hollingsheade in Barbados, 1657. [Minutes of the
Council of Barbados, 9/1657]

**DUVALL, JOHN,** from Waterford on the St George of
London, to Maryland in 1677.
[SPDom#19/393][MSA.LO.Patents#15/553]

**DWYER, CATE,** from Waterford on the St George of London,
to Maryland in 1677.
[SPDom#19/393][MSA.LO.Patents#15/553]

**DWYER, JAMES,** from Ireland, with his wife, two sons and
two daughters, settled in Beckwith, Ontario, on 14
August 1821. [PAO.MS154]

**EAGAN, LAUGHLIN,** from Waterford on the St George of
London, to Maryland in 1677. [SPDom#19/393]
[MSA.LO.Patents#15/553]

**ECKLIN, THOMAS,** from Ireland, a former corporal of the 5th
Regiment,with his wife, two sons and one daughter,
settled in Bathurst, Ontario, on 7 August 1817.
[PAO.MS154]

**EDGAR, ROBERT,** from Ireland, settled in Monaghan,
Newcastle, Ontario, on 28 May 1818. [PAO.MS154]

**EDWARDS, FRANCIS,** from Ireland, settled in Beckwith,
Ontario, on 4 September 1822. [PAO.MS154]

**EDWARDS, GEORGE,** from Ireland, settled in Beckwith,
Ontario, on 1 May 1820. [PAO.MS154]

**EDWARDS, Mrs NANCY,** a widow, from Ireland, settled in
Beckwith, Ontario, on 7 September 1822.
[PAO.MS154]

**EDWARDS, NOBLE,** from Ireland, settled in Cavan,
Newcastle, Ontario, on 13 September 1817.
[PAO.MS154]

**EDWARDS, RICHARD,** from Ireland, settled in Beckwith,
Ontario, on 30 November 1820. [PAO.MS154]

**EGAN, JOHN,** from Waterford on the St George of London,
to Maryland in 1677.
[SPDom#19/393][MSA.LO.Patents#15/553]

**ELLIOT, ADAM,** from Ireland, settled in Westminster,
London, Ontario, on 3 October 1817. [PAO.MS154]

**ELLIOT, JOHN,** a former Lieutenant of the Royal Marines,
land grant in Bathurst, Ontario, 18 September 1819.
[PAO.MS154]

**ELLIOT, NINIAN,** from Ireland, settled in Westminster,
London, Ontario, on 3 October 1817. [PAO.MS154]

**ELLIOT, WILLIAM,** from Ireland, settled in Cavan,
Newcastle, Ontario, on 12 October 1818. [PAO.MS154]

**ELLIS, NATHANIEL,** from Ireland, a former private of the
49th Regiment, with his wife, settled in Bathurst,
Ontario, on 10 September 1818. [PAO.MS154]

**ENGLISH, JAMES,** from Ireland, settled in Cavan,
Newcastle, Ontario, on 15 October 1818. [PAO.MS154]

**ENGLISH, JOAN,** from Youghal to Maryland on the
Encrease of Youghal, master Philip Popplestone, in
1679. [Dorchester Co. Patents, WC#129]
[MSA.Patents#20/184]

**ENGLISH, JOHN,** formerly a private of the 104th Regiment,
from Ireland, settled in Burgess, Ontario, on 22 August
1816. [PAO.MS154]

**ENGLISH, PATRICK,** an indentured servant who emigrated
from Limerick to America on the Industry of
Westhaven, master James Lowes, in March 1774.
[Hook pp, DU]

**ENGLISH, WALTER,** from Waterford on the St George of
London, to Maryland in 1677.
[SPDom#19/393][MSA.LO.Patents#15/553]

**ENGLISH, WILLIAM,** from Ireland, settled in March, Ontario,
on 20 August 1821. [PAO.MS154]

**ENRIGHT, THOMAS,** from Ireland, settled in Marlborough,
Ontario, on 14 August 1822. [PAO.MS154]

**ERWIN, FRANCIS,** an Irish indentured servant and blacksmith, absconded from George Plater, St Mary's County, Maryland, on 18 February 1759. [MdGaz#726]

**EVANS, JOHN,** emigrated from the Cove of Cork on the Hebe bound for Quebec on 8 July 1823, settled in Ontario. [PAO.MS154]

**EVANS, NICOLAS,** an indentured servant who emigrated from Belfast on the Bruerton of Liverpool, master John Fowler, to Philadedlphia in 1729. [PRONI#D354/71]

**EVATT, HENRY,** from Ireland, a former Lieutenant of the 21st Regiment, settled in Young, Ontario, 18 August 1818. [PAO.MS154]

**EVERIT, CHRISTOPHER,** from Waterford on the St George of London, to Maryland in 1677. [SPDom#19/393][MSA.LO.Patents#15/553]

**EWDALE, JOHN,** born around 1706, a carpenter and joiner/indentured servant who absconded from Thomas Snowden, near Patuxent Iron Works, Maryland, on 1 September 1751. [MdGaz#332]

**FAIR, ALEXANDER,** from Ireland, settled in Cavan, Newcastle, Ontario, on 16 February 1818. [PAO.MS154]

**FAIRBANKS, ROBERT,** a tailor, Balnecross, County Wexford, purchased land in West New Jersey in 1664. [NYGBR#30]

**FANNIN, ELLEN,** from Waterford on the St George of London, to Maryland in 1677. [SPDom#19/393][MSA.LO.Patents#15/553]

**FANNIN, PATRICK,** from Waterford on the St George of London, to Maryland in 1677. [SPDom#19/393][MSA.LO.Patents#15/553]

**FARGAR, THOMAS,** born 1743, Margaret born 1746, and James born 1764, arrived in South Carolina in January 1768 on the brigantine Chichester, master William Reid, from Belfast. [SCCJ.34.1]

**FARREL, EDWARD,** from Ireland, a former private of the 4th Dragoon Guards, with two sons, settled in Bathurst, Ontario, on 31 July 1817. [PAO.MS154]

**FARRELL, LAWRENCE,** born in Ireland during 1736, 5 feet 10 inches tall, a convict-indentured servant, absconded from the Baltimore ironworks, Maryland, on 17 July 1759, also on 25 March 1760. [MdGaz#741/777]

**FARRELL, WILLIAM,** 6 feet high, an Irish indentured servant/clothier and dyer who absconded from Anthony Strother in Fredericksburg, Virginia, on 20 June 1752. [VaGaz.17.7.1752]

**FARRELL, WILLIAM,** from Ireland, settled in Cavan, Newcastle, Ontario, on 3 October 1817. [PAO.MS154]

**FARRILL, THOMAS,** 5 feet 8 inches tall, a tanner from Ireland, an indentured servant who absconded from Miles Taylor in Richmond, Henrico County, Virginia, on 21 April 1774. [VaGaz.28.4.1774]

**FEAHINE, JOHN,** from Youghal to Maryland on the Encrease of Youghal, master Philip Popplestone, in 1679. [Dorchester Co. Patents, WC#129] [MSA.Patents#20/184]

**FERGUSON, GEORGE,** from Ireland, settled in Cavan, Newcastle, Ontario, on 22 August 1818. [PAO.MS154]

**FERRILL, FRANCIS,** a convict indentured servant who absconded from John Hammond and Robert Langford, Elk Ridge, Anne Arundel County, Maryland, on 22 June 1751. [MdGaz#324]

**FERRILL, FRANCIS,** born around 1702, an indentured servant who absconded from Neal Clark and John Welsh in Anne Arundel County, Maryland, on 30 March 1752. [MdGaz#365]

**FINDLAY, RICHARD,** arrived on the Mary and Bell on 15 July 1817, land grant in Beckwithwith, Ontario, 15 February 1818. [PAO.MS154]

**FINGLES, GEORGE,** from Waterford on the St George of London, to Maryland in 1677. [SPDom#19/393][MSA.LO.Patents#15/553]

**FINNARTY, JOHN,** formerly of the 4th Royal Veteran Battalion, with his wife, son and daughter, from Ireland, settled in Bathurst, Ontario, on 30 June 1817. [PAO.MS154]

**FINNELING, NICHOLAS,** a tailor and indentured servant who absconded from George Long in Maryland in April 1754. [MdGaz#468]

**FINNY, JAMES,** from Ireland, a former private of the 19th Dragoons, with his wife, son and daughter, settled in Elmsley, Ontario, on 23 October 1817. [PAO.MS154]

**FISHER, HUGH,** from Edenberry parish, County Down, settled in South Carolina before 1725. [vide Alexander Hutchison's will, probate 26 January 1725, Dublin Register of Deeds]

**FISHER, JAMES,** from Ireland, settled in Cavan, Newcastle, Ontario, on 14 October 1817. [PAO.MS154]

**FITZGERALD, CATE,** from Waterford on the St George of London, to Maryland in 1677. [SPDom#19/393][MSA.LO.Patents#15/553]

**FITZGERALD, JAMES,** from Ireland, formerly of the Royal Navy, settled in Beckwith, Ontario, on 9 September 1817. [PAO.MS154]

**FITZGERALD, JOHN,** born 1722, absconded from Charles Ridgely in Baltimore County, Maryland, in September 1752. [MdGaz#390]

**FITZGERALD, JOHN,** formerly a private of the Glengarry Fencibles, with his wife, from Ireland, settled in Burgess, Ontario, on 26 September 1816. [PAO.MS154]

**FITZGERALD, LUKE,** from Waterford on the St George of London, to Maryland in 1677. [SPDom#19/393][MSA.LO.Patents#15/553]

**FITZGERALD, MARGARET,** born 1801, from Rathcormac, County Cork, emigrated from Cove on the Stakesby bound for Quebec on 8 July 1823, settled in Ramsay township, Ontario. [PAO.prp]

**FITZGERALD, MORRIS,** from Waterford on the St George of London, to Maryland in 1677. [SPDom#19/393][MSA.LO.Patents#15/553]

**FITZGERALD, MORRIS,** from Youghal to Maryland on the Encrease of Youghal, master Philip Popplestone, in 1679. [Dorchester Co. Patents, WC#129][MSA.Patents#20/184]

**FITZGERALD, PATRICK,** a former corporal of the York Chasseurs, and his wife, land grant in Bathurst, Ontario, on 22 September 1819. [PAO.MS154]

**FITZGERALD, PATRICK,** from Ireland, late of the Prince of Wales's Chasseurs, settled in Beckwith, Ontario, on 10 October 1820. [PAO.MS154]

**FITZGERALD, THOMAS,** from Waterford on the St George of London, to Maryland in 1677. [SPDom#19/393][MSA.LO.Patents#15/553]

**FITZMAURICE, ULYSSES,** a former Lieutenant of the Canadian Fusiliers, from Ireland, settled in Bathurst, Ontario, on 30 June 1817. [PAO.MS154]

**FITZPATRICK, MARY,** an indentured servant who emigrated from Limerick to America on the Industry of Westhaven, master James Lowes, in March 1774. [Hook pp, DU]

**FITZSIMMONS, ULYSSES,** formerly a Lieutenant of the Canadian Fencibles, from Ireland, settled in Burgess, Ontario, on 19 September 1816. [PAO.MS154]

**FITZWILLIAMS, HUGH,** a farmer from Ireland, settled in Smith, Newcastle, Ontario, on 15 April 1819. [PAO.MS154]

**FLANAGAN, TERENCE,** born 1722, an Irish indentured servant who absconded from the Baltimore Iron Works on 20 May 1746. [MdGaz#57]

**FLARARTY, DARBY,** an indentured servant who absconded from the ship Anna at Lower Marlborough, Maryland, on 24 June 1751. [MdGaz#323]

**FLEMING, ANDREW,** possibly from County Tyrone, settled in Pennsylvania by 1758. [PRONI#T2493/1]

**FLEMING, ANDREW,** from Ireland, settled in Goulburn, Ontario, on 3 March 1822. [PAO.MS154]

**FLEMING, CHARLES,** with his wife and son, from Ireland, settled in Dalhousie, Ontario, on 8 September 1821. [PAO.MS154]

**FLEMING, JAMES,** an indentured servant who emigrated from Limerick to America on the Industry of Westhaven, master James Lowes, in March 1774. [Hook pp, DU]

**FLEMING, THOMAS,** possibly from County Tyrone, settled in Pennsylvania by 1758. [PRONI#T2493/1]

**FLEMING, WILLIAM,** born in County Monaghan during 1750, died in Charleston, South Carolina, on 6

February 1806, buried in the Old Scots Church there.
[Charleston g/s]

**FLINN, DANIEL,** from Ireland, settled in Ramsay, Ontario, on
10 May 1821. [PAO.MS154]

**FLINN, THOMAS,** with his wife and two daughters, from
Ireland, settled in Dalhousie, Ontario, on 11 March
1821. [PAO.MS154]

**FLOOD, OWEN,** with his wife and daughter, from Ireland,
settled in Dalhousie, Ontario, on 2 June 1821.
[PAO.MS154]

**FLOOD, PATRICK,** an Irish indentured servant and baker
who absconded from John Mitchell in Urbanna,
Middlesex County, Virginia, on 27 October 1738.
[VaGaz.10.3.1738]

**FLYNN, JAMES,** born 1792, with his wife Margaret born
1795, and children William born 1813, John born
1815, and Daniel born 1820, from Cork, emigrated
from Cove on the Stakesby to Quebec on 8 July 1823,
settled in Ramsay township, Ontario. [PAO.prp]

**FOLEY, DARBY,** from Ireland, a convict indentured servant
who absconded from John Fitzgerald in King William
County, Virginia, on 5 May 1745. [VaGaz.30.5.1745]

**FOLEY, DARBY,** from Ireland, settled in Cavan, Newcastle,
Ontario, on 21 May 1818. [PAO.MS154]

**FOLEY, JOHN,** formerly a private of the Glengarry
Fencibles, from Ireland, settled in Drummond, Ontario,
on 18 July 1816. [PAO.MS154]

**FOLEY, MICHAEL,** from Ireland, settled in Lanark, Ontario,
on 8 September 1821. [PAO.MS154]

**FOLEY, PATRICK,** with Helen, Mary, John, David, Patrick,
Michael and Helen, from Castle Lyons, County Cork,
emigrated from the Cove of Cork on the Hebe bound
for Quebec on 8 July 1823, settled in Ramsay, Ontario.
[PAO.prp]

**FOLLIS, JOHN,** from Ireland, settled in Cavan, Newcastle,
Ontario, on 1 December 1817. [PAO.MS154]

**FORSYTH, JAMES,** from Ireland, settled in Lanark, Ontario,
on 8 September 1821. [PAO.MS154]

**FOSTER, ELIZABETH,** from Youghal to Maryland on the
Encrease of Youghal, master Philip Popplestone, in

1679. [Dorchester Co. Patents, WC#129]
[MSA.Patents#20/184]

**FOSTER, GEORGE,** from Ireland, settled in Cavan,
Newcastle, Ontario, on 12 October 1818. [PAO.MS154]

**FOSTER, MATHIAS,** merchant, Dublin, purchased land in
West New Jersey in 1664. [NYGBR#30]

**FOSTER, ROBERT,** a yeoman from Ireland, settled in Cavan
Newcastle, Ontario, on 12 September 1818.
[PAO.MS154]

**FOWLER, JAMES,** from Ireland, settled in Smith, Newcastle,
Ontario, on 9 December 1819. [PAO.MS154]

**FOWLER, THOMAS,** born in Ireland during 1738, 5 feet 5
inches tall, thick set, dark eyes and a red complexion,
deserted from the Virginia Regiment on 2 June 1759.
[MdGaz#740]

**FOX, RICHARD K.,** son of James Fox {1814-1892} and
Margaret Fox, settled in New York. [Knock g/s, County
Down]

**FOY, PATRICK,** an indentured servant who emigrated from
Limerick to America on the Industry of Westhaven,
master James Lowes, in March 1774. [Hook pp, DU]

**FRANCIS, JOHN,** from Waterford on the St George of
London, to Maryland in 1677.
[SPDom#19/393][MSA.LO.Patents#15/553]

**FRANCIS, WILLIAM,** from Ireland, settled in Lanark,
Ontario, on 8 September 1821. [PAO.MS154]

**FRANCY, LAURIE,** with his wife and son, from Ireland,
landed from the Action, a brig, on 6 August 1817,
settled in Kitley, Ontario, on 6 October 1817. [PAO]

**FRASER, JOHN,** in Nelson, British Columbia, by 1899, son
of Thomas Fraser in Belfast and his wife Janet
Buchanan Dow who died 9 October 1870.
[NAS.SH.24.5.1899]

**FREELAND, JOHN,** from Ireland, settled in Toronto, Home,
Ontario, on 22 April 1819. [PAO.MS154]

**FREEMAN, PATRICK,** from Youghal to Maryland on the
Encrease of Youghal, master Philip Popplestone, in
1679. [Dorchester Co. Patents, WC#129]
[MSA.Patents#20/184]

**FRENCH, JOHN,** born 1799, with wife Mary born 1799,
daughter Sarah born 1821, from Mallow, County Cork,

emigrated from Cove on the Stakesby to Quebec on 8 July 1823, settled in Pakenham, Ontario. [PAO.prp]

FRITH, CHRISTOPHER, son of Christopher Frith {1779-1846} and Catherine Frith {1792-1838}, died in Ohio. [Knock g/s, County Down]

FRIZALL, JAMES, an indentured servant who emigrated from Belfast on the Bruerton of Liverpool, master John Fowler, to Philadelphia in 1729. [PRONI#D354/71]

FRIZALL, RICHARD, with his wife, landed from the Robert on 13 July 1821, settled in Shelbourne, Ontario, on 3 December 1821. [PAO]

FRIZALL, SUTTON, with his wife, landed from the Robert on 13 July 1821, settled in Shelbourne, Ontario, on 3 December 1821. [PAO]

FULLEN, PETER, from Ireland, late a private of the 27th Regiment, settled in Beckwith, Ontario, on 24 September 1822. [PAO]

FULTON, JAMES, from Ireland, late a corporal of the 12th Royal Veteran Battalion, with his wife and son, settled in Beckwith, Ontario, on 3 September 1820. [PAO.MS154]

GAIN, JOHN, from Ireland, late of the Royal Sappers, with his wife, two sons and two daughters, settled in Lanark, Ontario, on 1 November 1820. [PAO.MS154]

GALBRAITH, ANDREW, settled in Chester County, Pennsylvania, before 1724. [CCA.J.Davenport file]

GALLAGHER, HUGH, from Ireland, formerly of the 4th Royal Veteran Battalion, with his wife, settled in Drummond, Ontario, on 25 September 1817. [PAO.MS154]

GALLAGHER, JOHN, with his wife, two sons and one daughter, landed from the Douglas on 28 July 1821, settled in Bathurst, Ontario, on 3 December 1821. [PAO.MS154]

GALLAHOE, DANIEL, from Youghal to Maryland on the Encrease of Youghal, master Philip Popplestone, in 1679. [Dorchester Co. Patents, WC#129] [MSA.Patents#20/184]

GALVIN, DENNIS, born 1804, from Mallow, County Cork, emigrated from Cove on the Stakesby to Quebec on 8 July 1823, settled in Ramsay township, Ontario. [PAO.prp]

**GAMMEL, JOHN,** from Ireland, settled in Ramsay, Ontario, on 6 May 1821. [PAO.MS154]

**GANNON, JAMES,** born in Ireland during 1841, a laborer who emigrated via Glasgow, Scotland, on the S.S.Manitoban to Halifax, Nova Scotia, in April 1881. [PANS]

**GARLAND, NICHOLAS,** from Ireland, settled in Beckwith, Ontario, on 29 November 1821. [PAO.MS154]

**GARRAN, ROBERT,** an indentured servant who emigrated from Belfast on the Bruerton of Liverpool, master John Fowler, to Philadelphia in 1729. [PRONI#D354/71]

**GARTLAND, JOHN,** from Ireland, settled in Beckwith, Ontario, on 23 August 1820. [PAO.MS154]

**GARVEY, ALEXANDER,** a former soldier then an indentured servant who absconded from Jane Jameson, Kent County, Maryland, in November 1755. [MdGaz#552]

**GARVIN, THOMAS,** from Ireland, settled in Goulburn, Ontario, on 13 August 1822. [PAO.MS154]

**GAVIN, THOMAS,** from Ireland, settled in Huntley, Ontario, on 23 August 1820. [PAO.MS154]

**GEAYTORY, FRANCIS,** from Ireland, settled in Dalhousie, Ontario, on 6 February 1821. [PAO.MS154]

**GELLIBURNE, THOMAS,** from Youghal to Maryland on the Encrease of Youghal, master Philip Popplestone, in 1679. [Dorchester Co. Patents, WC#129] [MSA.Patents#20/184]

**GERALD, MARGARET,** from Youghal to Maryland on the Encrease of Youghal, master Philip Popplestone, in 1679. [Dorchester Co. Patents, WC#129] [MSA.Patents#20/184]

**GIBSON, JOHN,** son of Andrew Gibson in Omagh, emigrated from Ireland to Philadelphia in 1788. [WCA]

**GIBSON, WILLIAM,** and his family, emigrated from Belfast to Charleston, South Carolina, in 1788. [WCA]

**GIFF, JOHN,** from Ireland, settled in Beckwith, Ontario, on 20 August 1820. [PAO.MS154]

**GILES, JANE.** from Waterford on the St George of London, to Maryland in 1677. [SPDom#19/393][MSA.LO.Patents#15/553]

**GILLESPIE, JOHN**, late of the Royal Sappers, with his wife and son, settled in Lanark, Ontario, 1 November 1820. [PAO.MS154]

**GILMOR, JAMES,** born 1752, a mill-wright from Ireland, emigrated from Port Greenock, Scotland, on the Isobella, master William McLennan, bound for Jamaica in July 1775. [PRO.T47/12]

**GILROY, GEORGE,** with his wife, two sons and one daughter, from Ireland, settled in Sherbrook, Ontario, on 24 January 1822. [PAO.MS154]

**GIRLINGS, LIONEL**, from Waterford on the St George of London, to Maryland in 1677.
[SPDom#19/393][MSA.LO.Patents#15/553]

**GLEASON, MICHAEL,** a former private of the Glengarry Fencibles, from Ireland, settled in Burgess, Ontario, on 30 June 1817. [PAO.MS154]

**GOOD, FRANCIS**, non-cupative will dated 26 November 1701, Westmoreland County, Virginia.

**GOOD, JOHN,** from Ireland, settled in Marlborough, Ontario, on 3 March 1822. [PAO.MS154]

**GOOD, WILLIAM,** from Ireland, settled in Marlborough, Ontario, on 12 August 1820. [PAO.MS154]

**GOODMAN, MOSES,** formerly a sergeant of the Canadian Fencibles, from Ireland, settled in Burgess, Ontario, on 22 August 1816. [PAO.MS154]

**GORDON, JAMES,** a tailor from Ireland, settled in Cavan, Newcastle, Ontario, on 27 October 1818. [PAO.MS154]

**GORDON, JOHN,** from Ireland, settled in Goulburn, Ontario, on 25 February 1820. [PAO.MS154]

**GORDON, ROBERT,** emigrated from Ireland to Pennsylvania in 1769, settled at Fort Penn and later in Albany, New York, Loyalist in 1776, moved to Quebec. [PRO.AO12.28.374]

**GORDON, WILLIAM,** from Ireland, settled in Goulburn, Ontario, on 30 September 1821. [PAO.MS154]

**GOREMOND, EDMOND**, from Youghal to Maryland on the Encrease of Youghal, master Philip Popplestone, in 1679. [Dorchester Co. Patents, WC#129] [MSA.Patents#20/184]

**GORMAN, CORNELIUS,** late of the Royal Sappers, and his son, settled in Lanark, Ontario, 1 November 1820. [PAO.MS154]

**GORMAN, JOHN,** a yeoman from Ireland, settled in Smith, Newcastle, Ontario, on 9 November 1818. [PAO.MS154]

**GOTHIER, JOHN,** from Ireland, settled in Brock, Ontario, on 9 May 1818. [PAO.MS154]

**GOUGH, PATRICK,** from Ireland, settled in Cavan, Newcastle, Ontario, on 2 May 1818. [PAO.MS154]

**GOUGH, THOMAS,** from Ireland, settled in Cavan, Newcastle, Ontario, on 2 May 1818. [PAO.MS154]

**GOURLAY, GAWIN,** born 1805, son of Thomas Gourlay {1769-1844} and Elizabeth Gourlay {1767-1842}, died in New Orleans on 5 April 1836. [Comber g/s]

**GRACE, JOHN,** from Ireland, a former private of the 4th Royal Veteran Battalion, settled in Drummond, Ontario, on 25 September 1817. [PAO.MS154]

**GRAHAM, ARTHUR,** from Ireland, settled in Cavan, Newcastle, Ontario, on 3 August 1818. [PAO.MS154]

**GRAHAM, CHRISTOPHER,** from Ireland, settled in Goulburn, Ontario, on 30 July 1821. [PAO.MS154]

**GRAHAM, HENRY,** from Ireland, a former Lieutenant of the 103rd Regiment, with his wife, settled in Drummond, Ontario, on 21 September 1818. [PAO.MS154]

**GRAHAM, HUGH,** with his wife, five sons and one daughter, from Ireland, settled in Lanark, Ontario, on 8 September 1821. [PAO.MS154]

**GRAHAM, J.,** from Ireland, settled in Cavan, Newcastle, Ontario, on 4 October 1817. [PAO.MS154]

**GRAHAM, JACOB,** from Ireland, settled in March, Ontario, on 10 May 1822. [PAO.MS154]

**GRAHAM, JOHN,** from Ireland, settled in Huntley, Ontario, on 24 July 1822. [PAO.MS154]

**GRAHAM, NOBLE,** from Ireland, settled in Lanark, Ontario, on 8 September 1821. [PAO.MS154]

**GRAHAM, ROBERT,** from Ireland, settled in Cavan, Newcastle, Ontario, on 4 October 1817. [PAO.MS154]

**GRAHAM, THOMAS,** from Ireland, settled in Huntley, Ontario, on 12 July 1822. [PAO.MS154]

**GRAMLEY, MICHAEL,** born 1726, an Irish indentured servant who absconded from Thomas Williams in Prince William County, Virginia, on 2 June 1751. [VaGaz.18.7.1751]

**GRAY, CHARLES,** a blacksmith from Ireland, settled in Smith, Newcastle, Ontario, on 9 November 1818. [PAO.MS154]

**GRAY, JOHN,** a carpenter from Ireland, settled in Smith, Newcastle, Ontario, on 9 November 1818. [PAO.MS154]

**GREEN, ALICE,** from Youghal to Maryland on the Encrease of Youghal, master Philip Popplestone, in 1679. [Dorchester Co. Patents, WC#129] [MSA.Patents#20/184]

**GREEN, JOHN,** an indentured servant who emigrated from Belfast on the Bruerton of Liverpool, master John Fowler, to Philadelphia in 1729. [PRONI#D354/71]

**GREEN, JOHN,** born 1791, with Katherine Green born 1801, Thomas Green born 1793, Bustard Green born 1798, Anne Green born 1800, Rose Green born 1799, William Green born 1801, George Green born 1803, and Abigail Green born 1798, from Castletownroche, County Cork, emigrated voa Cove on the Stakesby to Quebec on 8 July 1823, settled in Pakenham, Ontario. [PAO.prp]

**GREENLEES, ANDREW,** from Magheramorne, County Antrim, emigrated to America in 1852, settled in Plattsburg, New York. [PRONI#T2046]

**GREENLEES, JAMES,** an indentured servant who emigrated from Belfast on the Bruerton of Liverpool, master John Fowler, to Philadelphia in 1729. [PRONI#D354/71]

**GREEVE, JOHN,** of Lurgan, Ireland, applied for a land grant of 20,000 acres in Nova Scotia, 5 February 1770. [JCTP.1770.25]

**GREGG, MICHAEL,** born 1800, from Conna, County Cork, emigrated from Cove on the Stakesby to Quebec on 8 July 1823, settled in Pakenham, Ontario. [PAO.prp]

**GREGG, WILLIAM,** born 1789, with his wife Fanny born 1789, and children William born 1818, Mary born 1819, and Eliza born 1822, from Conna, County Cork,

emigrated from Cove on the Stakesby to Quebec on 8
July 1823, settled in Pakenham, Ontario. [PAO.prp]

**GREGORY, WILLIAM,** sr., from Waterford on the St George
of London, to Maryland in 1677.
[SPDom#19/393][MSA.LO.Patents#15/553]

**GREVILLE, WILLIAM,** from Ireland, settled in Beckwith,
Ontario, on 20 March 1820. [PAO.MS154]

**GRIFFIN, ANNE,** an indentured servant who emigrated from
Limerick to America on the Industry of Westhaven,
master James Lowes, in March 1774. [Hook pp, DU]

**GRIFFIN, MARY,** an indentured servant who emigrated from
Limerick to America on the Industry of Westhaven,
master James Lowes, in March 1774. [Hook pp, DU]

**GRIFFIN, JOHN,** born around 1723, an Irish indentured
servant and weaver, absconded from David Long a
blacksmith in Annapolis, Maryland, on 13 October
1747. [MdGaz#130]

**GRIFFITH, EDWARD,** from Ireland, formerly of the 10<sup>th</sup>
Regiment, settled in Elmsly, Ontario, 23 February
1818. [PAO.MS154]

**GRIFFITH, EDWARD,** from Ireland, a former private of the
10<sup>th</sup> Regiment, settled in Beckwith, Ontario, on 13
October 1817. [PAO.MS154]

**GRIFFITHS, EVAN,** formerly a private of the 81<sup>st</sup> Regiment,
from Ireland, settled in Drummond, Ontario, on 21
October 1816. [PAO.MS154]

**GRIMMELL, HONOR,** an indentured servant who emigrated
from Limerick to America on the Industry of
Westhaven, master James Lowes, in March 1774.
[Hook pp, DU]

**GUBBINS, WILLIAM,** born 1783, from Castletownroche,
County Cork, emigrated from Cork on the Stakesby to
Quebec on 8 July 1823, settled in Ramsay township,
Ontario. [PAO.prp]

**GUIN, JAMES,** born 1709, a shoemaker, deserted from the
Virginia Regiment in 1754. [MdGaz#467]

**GUIRON, THOMAS,** formerly an army private, from Ireland,
settled in Drummond, Ontario, on 14 October 1816.
[PAO.MS154]

**GURKINSON, WILLIAM,** from Ireland, settled in Goulburn,
Ontario, on 18 September 1822. [PAO.MS154]

**HADE, JOHN,** from Ireland, landed from the Saltham on 1 August 1817, settled in Landsdowne, Ontario, on 6 October 1817. [PAO.MS154]

**HAGARTY, JOHN,** a former gunner of the Royal Artillery, with his wife and son, from Ireland, settled in Bathurst, Ontario, on 30 June 1817. [PAO.MS154]

**HAILEY, THOMAS,** born 1725, 5 feet 8 inches tall, an Irish indentured servant who absconded from Dr William Lynn in Fredericksburg, Virginia, on 20 July 1746. [MdGaz#76][VaGaz.7.8.1746]

**HALFPENNY, JOHN,** an Irish indentured servant and husbandman who absconded from Thomas Turner in King George County, Virginia, on 2 April 1739. [VaGaz.13.4.1739]

**HALL, GEORGE,** from Ireland, settled in Cavan, Newcastle, Ontario, on 23 October 1817. [PAO.MS154]

**HALL, JAMES,** a former corporal of the Sappers and Miners, with his wife, two sons and two daughters, land grant in Burgess, Ontario, 18 September 1819. [PAO.MS154]

**HALL, WILLIAM,** from Ireland, settled in March, Ontario, on 23 August 1820. [PAO.MS154]

**HALLENAN, JOHN,** indentured servant who emigrated from Limerick to America on the Industry of Westhaven, master James Lowes, in March 1774. [Hook pp, DU]

**HALLISON, EDMOND,** from Waterford on the St George of London, to Maryland in 1677. [SPDom#19/393][MSA.LO.Patents#15/553]

**HALLORAN, CATHER,** from Youghal to Maryland on the Encrease of Youghal, master Philip Popplestone, in 1679. [Dorchester Co. Patents, WC#129] [MSA.Patents#20/184]

**HALPEN, PETER,** born 1722, an Irish indentured servant/staymaker and tailor who absconded from Joseph Simpson in Richmond County, Virginia, during September 1752. [VaGaz.6.10.1752]

**HAMBLETON, JOHN,** an Irish indentured servant and carpenter who absconded from Dr Anthony Stafford in Nansemond County, Virginia, on 17 May 1738. [VaGaz.17.5.1738]

**HAMILTON, JOHN,** sr., a weaver from Ireland, settled in Cavan, Newcastle, Ontario, on 3 October 1818. [PAO.MS154]

**HAMILTON, JOHN,** jr, son of Alexander Hamilton, from Ireland, settled in Cavan, Newcastle, Ontario, on 3 October 1818. [PAO.MS154]

**HAMOND, HENRY,** from Ireland, settled in Lanark, Ontario, on 8 September 1821. [PAO.MS154]

**HANNAH, WILLIAM**, from Waterford on the St George of London, to Maryland in 1677. [SPDom#19/393][MSA.LO.Patents#15/553]

**HARDING, ROBERT**, from Dublin, settled in New England around 1633, returned to Ireland in 1653. [Cal.SPCol.1574-1660, fo.466]

**HARDING, WILLIAM**, emigrated to Georgia in 1768, Loyalist militia captain, died 1786. [PRO.AO13.35.391]

**HARFORD, PATRICK,** born 1727, a convict indentured servant, absconded from John Ridgeley's Plantation, Elk Ridge, Maryland, on 16 June 1748. [MdGaz#68]

**HARGE, WILLIAM**, from Youghal to Maryland on the Encrease of Youghal, master Philip Popplestone, in 1679. [Dorchester Co. Patents, WC#129] [MSA.Patents#20/184]

**HARGREAVES, ELIZABETH**, from Waterford on the St George of London, to Maryland in 1677. [SPDom#19/393][MSA.LO.Patents#15/553]

**HARGREAVES, JOHN**, from Waterford on the St George of London, to Maryland in 1677. [SPDom#19/393][MSA.LO.Patents#15/553]

**HARPER, ALEXANDER,** from Ireland, settled in March, Ontario, on 3 August 1822. [PAO.MS154]

**HARRIS, MICHAEL,** from Ireland, a Church of England minister, with his wife, settled in Bath, Ontario, on 24 September 1822. [PAO.MS154]

**HARRISON, HENRY,** an Irish indentured servant who absconded from Williamsburg, Virginia, during 1751. [VaGaz.8.8.1751]

**HART, JOSEPH,** from Ireland, settled in Ramsay, Ontario, on 10 May 1822. [PAO.MS154]

**HART, WILLIAM**, an Irish convict indentured servant, absconded from William Dames in Chester Town,

Maryland, in August 1746.
[MdGaz#69][VaGaz.28.8.1746]

**HARTAGANE, TIMOTHY**, from Youghal to Maryland on the Encrease of Youghal, master Philip Popplestone, in 1679. [Dorchester Co. Patents, WC#129] [MSA.Patents#20/184]

**HARVEY, JACOB,** a Quaker merchant from Limerick, settled in New York around 1816. [TCD#MS3641]

**HATHORN, JOHN,** born 1714, Elizabeth born 1723, Adam born 1745, James born 1747, John born 1750, Mary born 1751, Robert born 1753, Joseph born 1755, Benjamin born 1760, and Elizabeth born 1764, arrived in South Carolina in January 1768 on the brigantine Chichester, master William Reid, from Belfast. [SCCJ.34.1]

**HAUGHIEREN, JOHN**, from Youghal to Maryland on the Encrease of Youghal, master Philip Popplestone, in 1679. [Dorchester Co. Patents, WC#129] [MSA.Patents#20/184]

**HAVIOGHTEN, WILLIAM,** an Irish shoemaker and indentured servant, absconded from Mary Mahawne, Back River Neck, Baltimore County, Maryland, in October 1745. [MdGaz#25]

**HAWKINS, JOHN**, from Waterford on the St George of London, to Maryland in 1677. [SPDom#19/393][MSA.LO.Patents#15/553]

**HAWKINS, ROBERT**, from Youghal to Maryland on the Encrease of Youghal, master Philip Popplestone, in 1679. [Dorchester Co. Patents, WC#129] [MSA.Patents#20/184]

**HAWKINS, WILLIAM,** from Ireland, settled in Ramsay, Ontario, on 10 May 1821. [PAO.MS154]

**HAY, DAVID,** from Ireland, settled in Cavan, Newcastle, Ontario, on 3 October 1817. [PAO.MS154]

**HAYES, JAMES,** an indentured servant who emigrated from Limerick to America on the Industry of Westhaven, master James Lowes, in March 1774. [Hook pp, DU]

**HAYES, WILLIAM,** from Ireland, settled in Huntley, Ontario, on 27 November 1820. [PAO.MS154]

**HAYNES, MARGARET**, from Waterford on the St George of London, to Maryland in 1677.
[SPDom#19/393][MSA.LO.Patents#15/553]

**HAYS, THOMAS**, from Ireland, late of the Prince of Wales's Chasseurs, settled in Beckwith, Ontario, on 10 October 1820. [PAO.MS154]

**HAZLEWOOD, JOHN,** from Ireland, settled in Goulburn, Ontario, on 30 June 1822. [PAO.MS154]

**HAZLEWOOD, WILLIAM,** from Ireland, settled in March, Ontario, on 2 November 1822. [PAO.MS154]

**HEAGARTY, TIMOTHY,** from Ireland, settled in Marlborough, Ontario, on 2 November 1822. [PAO.MS154]

**HEALY, PATRICK,** born 1783, with wife Abbey born 1783, and children Mary born 1803, Dennis born 1805, James born 1808, and Margaret born 1818, from Fermoy, County Cork, emigrated from Cove on the Stakesby to Quebec on 8 July 1823, settled in Ramsay township, Ontario. [PAO.prp]

**HEALY, WILLIAM,** sr., from Ireland, settled in Goulburn, Ontario, on 1 January 1820. [PAO.MS154]

**HEALY, WILLIAM,** jr., from Ireland, settled in Goulburn, Ontario, on 1 February 1820. [PAO.MS154]

**HEARBOTTLE, WILLIAM,** from Waterford on the St George of London, to Maryland in 1677.
[SPDom#19/393][MSA.LO.Patents#15/553]

**HECKING, THOMAS**, a sailor, ran away from the sloop Sally, master Thomas Askew, in Annapolis, Maryland, on 14 July 1751. [MdGaz#325]

**HENDERSON, ALEXANDER,** born in Monaghan during 1800, died in Charleston, South Carolina, on 4 March 1826, buried in the Old Scots Church there.
[Charleston g/s]

**HENDERSON, DAVID,** from Waterford on the St George of London, to Maryland in 1677.
[SPDom#19/393][MSA.LO.Patents#15/553]

**HENDERSON, JACOB,** a minister, sent to Virginia on 1 July 1710, returned, then sent to Newcastle, Pennsylvania, on 24 July 1712, died on 19 January 1735. [EMA#33]

**HENDERSON, JAMES,** from Ireland, settled in Goulburn, Ontario, on 20 October 1820. [PAO.MS154]

**HENDERSON, ROBERT,** from Ireland, formerly of the 9th Dragoons, settled in Bathurst, Ontario, on 2 October 1817. [PAO.MS154]

**HENDREN, JOHN,** an indentured servant who emigrated from Belfast on the Bruerton of Liverpool, master John Fowler, to Philadelphia in 1729. [PRONI#D354/71]

**HENDREN, WILLIAM,** an indentured servant who emigrated from Belfast on the Bruerton of Liverpool, master John Fowler, to Philadelphia in 1729. [PRONI#D354/71]

**HENERY, THOMAS,** from Youghal to Maryland on the Encrease of Youghal, master Philip Popplestone, in 1679. [Dorchester Co. Patents, WC#129] [MSA.Patents#20/184]

**HENLEY, JOHN,** late of the Royal Sappers, with his wife and 3 daughters, settled in Lanark, Ontario, 1 November 1820. [PAO.MS154]

**HENNESSEY, CATHERINE,** from Youghal to Maryland on the Encrease of Youghal, master Philip Popplestone, in 1679. [Dorchester Co. Patents, WC#129] [MSA.Patents#20/184]

**HENNING, JAMES,** born 1750, arrived in South Carolina in January 1768 on the brigantine Chichester, master William Reid, from Belfast. [SCCJ.34.1]

**HENNISSY, THOMAS,** born 1780, with children Thomas born 1804, Honora born 1807, Mary born 1808, and Elisa born 1811, from Castlewrixon, County Cork, emigrated from Cove on the Stakesby to Quebec on 8 July 1823, settled in Ramsay township, Ontario. [PAO.prp]

**HENRY, ROBERT,** a former private of the 4th Royal Veterans, with his wife and two sons, from Ireland, settled in Bathurst, Ontario, on 24 July 1817. [PAO.MS154]

**HENRY, WILLIAM,** emigrated from Killeleagh, County Down, to America in 1770, settled in Chester County, Pennsylvania, Loyalist in 1776, returned to Ireland. [PRO.AO12.43.328]

**HERRILE, FRANCIS,** an indentured servant who absconded from John Hammond, Elk Ridge, Maryland, in July 1750. [MdGaz#275]

**HEWETSON, HUGH,** from Ireland, settled in Goulburn, Ontario, on 24 October 1822. [PAO.MS154]

**HICKEY, THOMAS,** from Ireland, settled in Monaghan, Newcastle, Ontario, on 17 November 1817. [PAO.MS154]

**HICKEY, WILLIAM,** from Michelstown, County Cork, emigrated from the Cove of Cork on the Hebe bound for Quebec on 8 July 1823, settled in Ramsay township, Ontario. [PAO.prp]

**HICKY, JOHN,** an indentured servant who emigrated from Limerick to America on the Industry of Westhaven, master James Lowes, in March 1774. [Hook pp, DU]

**HIGGINS, THOMAS,** from Ireland, settled in March, Ontario, on 23 August 1820. [PAO.MS154]

**HIGHLAND, JOHN,** sr., from Ireland, settled in Cavan, Newcastle, Ontario, on 14 October 1817. [PAO.MS154]

**HIGHLAND, JOHN,** jr., from Ireland, settled in Cavan, Newcastle, Ontario, on 14 October 1817. [PAO.MS154]

**HIGHLAND, ROBERT,** from Ireland, settled in Cavan, Newcastle, Ontario, on 21 September 1817. [PAO.MS154]

**HIGWOOD, ROBERT,** with his wife, son and two daughters, from Ireland, landed from the Mary Ann, on 8 August 1817, settled in Yonge, Ontario, on 16 September 1817. [PAO.MS154]

**HILL, JOHN,** from Ireland, settled in Monaghan, Newcastle, Ontario, on 28 April 1818. [PAO.MS154]

**HILL, THOMAS,** with his wife and daughter, from Ireland, landed from the Active on 8 August 1817, settled in Yonge, Ontario, on 15 September 1817. [PAO.prp]

**HILLARY, JOHN,** born 1752, arrived in South Carolina in January 1768 on the brigantine Chichester, master William Reid, from Belfast. [SCCJ.34.1]

**HILLIARD, JOHN,** from Waterford on the St George of London, to Maryland in 1677. [SPDom#19/393][MSA.LO.Patents#15/553]

**HOBBS, MURTHE,** from Ireland, landed from the General Moore on 8 August 1817, settled in Oxford, Ontario, on 6 October 1817. [PAO.MS154]

**HOBBS, PATRICK,** from Ireland, landed from the General Moore on 8 August 1817, settled in Oxford, Ontario, on 6 October 1817. [PAO.MS154]

**HOBBS, WILLIAM,** from Ireland, settled in Goulburn, Ontario, on 3 May 1822. [PAO.MS154]

**HOBSON, JOHN,** with one son and two daughters, from Ireland, landed from the Atlantic on 14 August 1817, settled in Oxford, Ontario, on 13 October 1817. [PAO.MS154]

**HODGE, FRANCIS,** born 1738, Elizabeth born 1739, Robert born 1759, Alexander born 1761, and John born 1763, arrived in South Carolina in January 1768 on the Chichester from Belfast. [SCCJ.34.1]

**HODGINS, JOHN,** from Ireland, settled in Goulburn, Ontario, on 2 September 1822. [PAO.MS154]

**HODGINS, MICHAEL,** from Ireland, settled in Goulburn, Ontario, on 2 September 1822. [PAO.MS154]

**HODGINS, RICHARD,** from Ireland, settled in Huntley, Ontario, on 14 August 1822. [PAO.MS154]

**HODGINS, THOMAS,** from Ireland, settled in Goulburn, Ontario, on 30 January 1820. [PAO.MS154]

**HODGINS, THOMAS,** from Ireland, settled in Huntley, Ontario, on 12 September 1821. [PAO.MS154]

**HOGAN, ANNE,** an indentured servant who emigrated from Limerick to America on the Industry of Westhaven, master James Lowes, in March 1774. [Hook pp, DU]

**HOGAN, DENNIS,** from Ireland, settled in Huntley, Ontario, on 30 August 1821. [PAO.MS154]

**HOGAN, DOMINICK,** an Irish indentured servant, absconded from Benjamin Tasker and Company, Patapsco Iron Works, Baltimore County, Maryland, on 25 June 1745. [MdGaz#14]

**HOGAN, JOHN,** from Ireland, a former soldier of the 58th Regiment, with his wife, son and two daughters, settled in Drummond, Ontario, on 23 October 1817. [PAO.NS154]

**HOGAN, TARTY,** from Waterford on the St George of London, to Maryland in 1677. [SPDom#19/393][MSA.LO.Patents#15/553]

**HOLBROOK, EDWARD,** from Ireland, settled in Beckwith, Ontario, on 30 November 1822. [PAO.MS154]

**HOLBROOK, THOMAS,** from Ireland, settled in Beckwith, Ontario, on 30 June 1822. [PAO.MS154]

**HOLLAM, JOHN,** from Waterford on the St George of London, to Maryland in 1677. [SPDom#19/393][MSA.LO.Patents#15/553]

**HOLLON, WILLIAM,** born around 1723, an Irish indentured servant, a blacksmith, who absconded from Samuel Howard in Annapolis, Maryland, on 20 April 1747. [MdGaz#104]

**HOLMES, WILLIAM,** son of William Holmes in Tullygoney, Benburb, County Tyrone, settled in Silver Bluerbluff near Pensacola, West Florida, by 1777. [PRONI#D1782/2]

**HOPKINS, EDWARD,** from Ireland, settled in Lanark, Ontario, on 8 September 1821. [PAO.MS154]

**HORAGAN, JOAN,** an indentured servant who emigrated from Limerick to America on the Industry of Westhaven, master James Lowes, in March 1774. [Hook pp, DU]

**HORAN, MICHAEL,** from Mallow, County Cork, emigrated from the Cove of Cork on the Hebe bound for Quebec on 8 July 1823, settled in Ramsay township, Ontario. [PAO.prp]

**HORNER, JAMES,** son of Thomas Horner in Newtown Limavady, County Londonderry, settled in Philadelphia in 1801. [PRONI#T1592/2]

**HOUGHTON, ANDREW,** with his wife and son, landed from the Sisters on 26 June 1820, settled in Beckwith, Ontario, on 4 December 1821. [PAO.MS154]

**HOUSTON, JOHN,** from Ireland, settled in Cavan, Newcastle, Ontario, on 12 May 1818. [PAO.MS154]

**HOUSTON, WILLIAM,** from Ireland, settled in Goulburn, Ontario, on 18 September 1822. [PAO.MS154]

**HOY, HUGH KENNEDY,** from Dublin, a merchant in New York, probate 7 April 1768 New York.

**HUGHES, BILLY,** an Irish indentured servant who absconded from Thomas Dansie in King William County, Virginia, in 1751. [VaGaz.9.5.1751]

**HUGHES, DAVID,** from Waterford on the St George of London, to Maryland in 1677. [SPDom#19/393][MSA.LO.Patents#15/553]

**HUGHES, JAMES,** landed from the Neptune on 2 July 1821, settled in Drummond, Ontario, on 4 December 1821. [PAO.MS154]

**HUGHES, JOHN,** formerly a private of the 6<sup>th</sup> Regiment, from Ireland, settled in Drummond, Ontario, on 14 October 1816. [PAO.MS154]

**HUGHES, JOHN,** a former Corporal of the Royal Artillery, with his wife and daughter, from Ireland, settled in Drummond, Ontario, on 31 March 1817. [PAO.MS154]

**HUGHES, JOHN,** from Ireland, formerly a Corporal of the Royal Artillery, settled in Drummond, Ontario, 26 April 1817. [PAO.MS154]

**HUGHES, JOHN,** from Ireland, settled in Ramsay, Ontario, on 1 October 1821. [PAO.MS154]

**HUGHES, OWEN,** with his wife and two sons, from Ireland, settled in Dalhousie, Ontario, on 2 June 1821. [PAO.MS154]

**HUNTER, JAMES,** from Ireland, settled in Cavan, Newcastle, Ontario, on 6 September 1817. [PAO.MS154]

**HUNTER, RICHARD,** a tanner, Dublin, purchased land in West New Jersey in 1664. [NYGBR#30]

**HUNTER, WILLIAM,** born 1771 in County Antrim, settled in Charleston, South Carolina, in 1788, died there on 18 September 1805, buried in the Old Scots Church there. [Charleston g/s]

**HUNTER, WILLIAM,** from Ireland, settled in Marlborough, Ontario, on 2 November 1822. [PAO.MS154]

**HUSBAND, JOHN,** from Ireland, settled in Cavan, Newcastle, Ontario, on 10 June 1818. [PAO.MS154]

**HUSTON, JOHN,** from Ireland, settled in Cavan, Newcastle, Ontario, on 10 February 1818. [PAO.MS154]

**HUSTON, ROBERT,** from Ireland, settled in Cavan, Newcastle, Ontario, on 10 February 1818. [PAO.MS154]

**HYDE, ANDREW,** an indentured servant who emigrated from Limerick to America on the Industry of Westhaven, master James Lowes, in March 1774. [Hook pp, DU]

**HYDE, JOHN,** born around 1712, an Irish indentured servant, absconded from T. Stansbury, Baltimore County, Maryland, on 3 March 1747. [MdGaz#99]

**IRELAND, MARY,** from Youghal to Maryland on the Encrease of Youghal, master Philip Popplestone, in 1679. [Dorchester Co. Patents, WC#129] [MSA.Patents#20/184]

**IRETON, JOHN,** with his wife, two sons and two daughters, from Ireland, settled in Lanark, Ontario, on 8 September 1821. [PAO.MS154]

**IRETON, THOMS,** with his wife and children, from Ireland, settled in Lanark, Ontario, on 12 September 1821. [PAO.MS154]

**IRWIN, FRANCES,** 5 feet 9 inches, an Irish indentured servant and blacksmith, absconded from Samuel Canby in Loudoun County, Virginia, on 14 May 1775. [VaGaz.8.6.1775]

**IRWIN, GEORGE,** from Ireland, settled in Huntley, Ontario, on 10 September 1821. [PAO.MS154]

**IRWIN, HUGH,** from Ireland, settled in Beckwith, Ontario, on 10 September 1821. [PAO.MS154]

**IRWIN, JOHN,** born 30 September 1787 in County Fermanagh, emigrated to USA in 1800, settled in Iredell County, North Carolina, a merchant in Charlotte by 1809, married Mary Patton, died in Charlotte on 18 July 1860. [North Carolina Presbyterian, 11.8.1860]

**IVORY, THOMAS,** born 1729, a marble cutter and indentured servant, immigrated into Maryland from Ireland in 1754, absconded from the Baltimore Iron Works in March 1756. [MdGaz#570]

**JACKSON, JAMES,** from Ireland, settled in Cavan, Newcastle, Ontario, on 3 August 1818. [PAO.MS154]

**JACKSON, LANCELOT,** from Ireland, settled in Lanark, Ontario, on 17 September 1821. [PAO.MS154]

**JACKSON, MARSHALL,** from Ireland, settled in Dalhousie, Ontario, on 17 September 1821. [PAO.MS154]

**JACKSON, THOMAS,** with his wife and two daughters, from Ireland, settled in Lanark, Ontario, on 25 January 1821. [PAO.MS154]

**JACOB, MARGARET**, from Waterford on the St George of London, to Maryland in 1677. [SPDom#19/393][MSA.LO.Patents#15/553]

**JACOBS, THOMAS,** from Ireland, landed from the Mary Ann on 8 August 1817, settled in Yonge, Ontario, on 6 October 1817. [PAO.MS154]

**JACOBS, WILLIAM,** from Ireland, landed from the Mary Ann on 8 August 1817, settled in Yonge, Ontario, on 6 October 1817. [PAO.MS154]

**JAMES, EDWARD,** sr., with his wife, two sons and a daughter, from Ireland, settled in Drummond, Ontario, on 3 October 1817. [PAO.MS154]

**JAMES, EDWARD,** jr., with his wife, two sons and a daughter, from Ireland, settled in Drummond, Ontario, on 3 October 1817. [PAO.MS154]

**JAMES, HENRY,** from Ireland, settled in Lanark, Ontario, on 17 September 1821. [PAO.MS154]

**JAMES, JOHN,** settled in Beckwith, Ontario, on 2 May 1821. [PAO.MS154]

**JAMES, PETER,** from Waterford on the St George of London, to Maryland in 1677. [SPDom#19/393][MSA.LO.Patents#15/553]

**JENNINGS, JOHN,** from Ireland, formerly of the Royal Artillery, settled in Beckwithwith, Ontario, 28 March 1818. [PAO.MS154]

**JESSOP, FRANCIS,** from Kilfinnane, County Limerick, emigrated from the Cove of Cork on the Hebe bound for Quebec on 8 July 1823, settled in Ramsay township, Ontario. [PAO.prp]

**JOHNSON, JOHN,** born in Dublin during 1718, 5 feet 10 inches tall, deserted from Captain Robert Hodgson's Independent Company in 1746. [VaGaz.27.6.1746]

**JOHNSON, JOHN,** sr. formerly a private of the Glengarry Fencibles, from Ireland, settled in Drummond, Ontario, on 16 July 1816. [PAO.MS154]

**JOHNSON, ROBERT,** sr., from Ireland, settled in Cavan, Newcastle, Ontario, on 24 September 1817. [PAO.MS154]

**JOHNSON, ROBERT,** jr., from Ireland, settled in Cavan, Newcastle, Ontario, on 24 September 1817. [PAO.MS154]

**JOHNSTON, ABRAHAM,** from Ireland, settled in Goulburn, Ontario, on 5 September 1822. [PAO.MS154]

**JOHNSTON, EDWARD,** from Ireland, settled in Huntley, Ontario, on 10 September 1821. [PAO.MS154]

**JOHNSTON, JOB,** from Slaughabogy, parish of Maghera, County Londonderry, settled in Oxford, Pennsylvania, by 1765. [PRONI#T3700/1]

**JOHNSTON, MOSES,** possibly from Loughbrickland, County Down, settled in Northumberland County, Pennsylvania, by 1790. [PRONI#T3588/7]

**JOHNSTON, RICHARD,** a laborer from Ireland, settled in Cavan, Newcastle, Ontario, on 25 September 1818. [PAO.MS154]

**JOHNSTON, ROBERT,** from Ireland, settled in Beckwith, Ontario, on 20 October 1820. [PAO.MS154]

**JOHNSTON, ROBERT,** from Ireland, settled in Huntley, Ontario, on 24 August 1822. [PAO.MS154]

**JOHNSTON, WILLIAM,** born 1750, arrived in South Carolina in January 1768 on the brigantine Chichester, master William Reid, from Belfast. [SCCJ.34.1]

**JOLLY, MATTHEW,** born about 1723, an Irish indentured servant, absconded from Benjamin Tasker and Company, Patapsco Iron Works, Baltimore County, Maryland on 25 June 1745. [MdGaz#13]

**JONES, GEORGE,** a former private of the 4th Royal Veteran Battalion, from Ireland, settled in Burgess, Ontario, on 30 June 1817. [PAO.MS154]

**JONES, JOHN,** from Youghal to Maryland on the Encrease of Youghal, master Philip Popplestone, in 1679. [Dorchester Co. Patents, WC#129] [MSA.Patents#20/184]

**JONES, JOHN,** late of the Royal Sappers, with his wife, son and 3 daughters, settled in Lanark, Ontario, on 1 November 1820. [PAO.MS154]

**JONES, ROBERT,** from Ireland, settled in Cavan, Newcastle, Ontario, on 13 September 1817. [PAO.MS154]

**JOYNT, ANDREW,** from Ireland, settled in Goulburn, Marlborough, Ontario, on 29 September 1820. [PAO.MS154]

**KAYES, JOHN,** from Ireland, settled in Lanark, Ontario, on 25 May 1821. [PAO.MS154]

**KAYES, RICHARD,** from Ireland, settled in Lanark, Ontario, on 25 May 1821. [PAO.MS154]

**KEALLY, MARRIAH,** from Youghal to Maryland on the Encrease of Youghal, master Philip Popplestone, in 1679. [Dorchester Co. Patents, WC#129] [MSA.Patents#20/184]

**KEARNS, THOMAS,** a former corporal of the Royal Artillery, with his wife and two daughters, from Ireland, settled in Bathurst, Ontario, on 24 July 1817. [PAO.MS154]

**KEAYS, JAMES,** alias Murphy, 5 feet 5 inches tall, an Irish convict indentured servant and joiner who absconded from Charles Neilson in Prince George County, Virginia, on 2 April 1751. [VaGaz.4.4.1751]

**KEEFE, DANIEL,** an indentured servant who emigrated from Limerick to America on the Industry of Westhaven, master James Lowes, in March 1774. [Hook pp, DU]

**KEENAN, DANIEL,** probably from the parish of Ballyscullion, settled in Baltimore, Maryland, before 1849. [PRONI#T2279/1]

**KEHOE, JAMES,** from Ireland, a former private of the 49th Regiment, with his wife and two daughters, settled in Bathurst, Ontario, on 12 August 1817. [PAO.MS154]

**KELLY, BRYAN,** an Irish indentured servant and gardener who absconded from Daniel Hornby in Richmond County, Virginia, on 3 September 1737. [VaGen.14.10.1737]

**KELLY, GILES,** from Waterford on the St George of London, to Maryland in 1677. [SPDom#19/393][MSA.LO.Patents#15/553]

**KELLY, MICHAEL,** 5 feet 5 inches, and Margaret his wife, both Irish indentured servants who absconded from William Hayth in Bedford County, Virginia, in May 1771. [VaGaz.16.5.1771]

**KELLY, PATRICK,** a former private of the Glengarry Regiment, with his wife, from Ireland, settled in Drummond, Ontario, on 16 July 1816. [PAO.MS154]

**KELLY, PATRICK,** with his wife and daughter, from Ireland, settled in Lanark, Ontario, on 18 April 1821. [PAO.MS154]

**KELLY, PETER,** from Ireland, a former private of the 43$^{rd}$ Regiment, settled in Burgess, Ontario, on 9 August 1817. [PAO.MS154]

**KELLY, THOMAS,** immigrated before 1749, an indentured servant who absconded from Robert Evans, Cecil County, Maryland, on 24 February 1753. [MdGaz#409]

**KELLY, THOMAS,** from Ireland, a former soldier of the York Chasseurs, land grant in Bathurst, Ontario, 2 September 1819. [PAO.MS154]

**KEMP, WILLIAM,** from Ireland, settled in Goulburn, Ontario, on 30 January 1820. [PAO.MS154]

**KEMPT, JOHN,** from Ireland, settled in Goulburn, Ontario, on 31 January 1821. [PAO.MS154]

**KENEALY, MARY,** an indentured servant who emigrated from Limerick to America on the Industry of Westhaven, master James Lowes, in March 1774. [Hook pp, DU]

**KENNEDY, ARCHIBALD,** from Ireland, settled in Cavan, Ontario, on 9 September 1817. [PAO.MS154]

**KENNEDY, BRYAN,** from Ireland, settled in Marlborough, Ontario, on 24 August 1822. [PAO.MS154]

**KENNEDY, CATHER,** from Youghal to Maryland on the Encrease of Youghal, master Philip Popplestone, in 1679. [Dorchester Co. Patents, WC#129] [MSA.Patents#20/184]

**KENNEDY, DAVID,** from Ireland, settled in Huntley, Ontario, on 30 September 1821. [PAO.MS154]

**KENNEDY, HENRY,** from Ireland, settled in Goulburn, Ontario, on 16 September 1822. [PAO.MS154]

**KENNEDY, JAMES,** born 1746, arrived in South Carolina in January 1768 on the brigantine Chichester, master William Reid, from Belfast. [SCCJ.34.1]

**KENNEDY, JAMES W.,** born in 1812, son of John Kennedy in Belfast, died in Vicksburg, America, on 5 August 1838. [Shankill g/s, Belfast]

**KENNEDY, JOHN,** a trader in New York, probate 17 November 1767 New York

**KENNEDY, JOHN,** born in Ireland during 1749, an indentured servant who absconded from the Catherine, master Thomas Patton, in February 1775. [VaGaz.23.2.1775]

**KENNEDY, JOHN,** from Ireland, settled in Cavan, Newcastle, Ontario, on 13 September 1817. [PAO.MS154]

**KENNEDY, THOMAS,** born 1737, an indentured servant who absconded from William Jessop, collier, Baltimore iron Works, in April 1757. [MdGaz#604]

**KENNEDY, THOMAS,** from Ireland, settled in Huntley, Ontario, on 1 November 1822. [PAO.MS154]

**KENNEDY, TIMOTHY,** born 1798, from Charleville, County Cork, emigrated from Cove on the Stakesby on 8 July 1823, settled in Pakenham, Ontario. [PAO.prp]

**KENT, JAMES,** from Ireland, formerly a private of the 6th Regiment, settled in Beckwith, Ontario, 6 April 1818. [PAO.MS154]

**KENYON, JOSEPH,** an Irish indentured servant who absconded from John Canaday, Fairfax County, Virginia, on 29 June 1746. [VaGaz.24.7.1746]

**KEOGH, OWEN,** with his wife, son and daughter, from Ireland, settled in Lanark, Ontario, on 17 October 1821. [PAO.MS154]

**KERFORD, SAMUEL,** from Ireland, settled in Beckwith, Ontario, on 30 January 1820. [PAO.MS154]

**KERR, JOHN,** settled in Pittsburgh, Alleghany County, Pennsylvania, by 1843. [PRONI#MIC144/1/3]

**KEYES, THOMAS,** from Ireland, settled in Goulburn, Ontario, on 30 November 1820. [PAO.MS154]

**KIDD, ADAM,** born 1802 in County Londonderry, a poet, died in Quebec on 5 July 1831. [GM.101.477]

**KIDD, GEORGE,** from Ireland, settled in Goulburn, Ontario, on 12 August 1822. [PAO.MS154]

**KIDD, THOMAS,** from Ireland, settled in Beckwith, Ontario, on 30 August 1821. [PAO.MS154]

**KIDD, WILLIAM,** from Ireland, settled in Beckwith, Ontario, on 30 August 1821. [PAO.MS154]

**KIDNEY, JAMES,** from Ireland, late of the Royal Sappers, with his wife and son, settled in Lanark, Ontario, on 1 November 1820. [PAO.MS154]

**KILDUFF, ROBERT,** from Ireland, settled in Huntley, Ontario, on 30 November 1823. [PAO.MS154]

**KILFORD, JOHN,** from Ireland, settled in Beck, Ontario, on 29 November 1821. [PAO.MS154]

**KILLAM, THOMAS**, from Waterford on the St George of London, to Maryland in 1677. [SPDom#19/393][MSA.LO.Patents#15/553]

**KILLEEN, DENIS,** from Ireland, settled in March, Ontario, on 23 August 1820. [PAO.MS154]

**KILPATRICK, RICHARD,** from Ireland, settled in Cavan, Newcastle, Ontario, on 7 October 1818. [PAO.MS154]

**KINCHLER, PETER,** 5 feet 5 inches tall, an Irish indentured servant who absconded from Robert Beedles in Orange County, Virginia, and was imprisoned in Augusta County jail in October 1771. [VaGaz.31.10.1751]

**KING, ARTHUR**, from Waterford on the St George of London, to Maryland in 1677. [SPDom#19/393][MSA.LO.Patents#15/553]

**KING, JOHN,** from Waterford on the St George of London, to Maryland in 1677. [SPDom#19/393][MSA.LO.Patents#15/553]

**KING, ROBERT DUNCAN,** born during 1816, eldest son of Captain J. D. King in Waterford, died in Port au Prince, Haiti, on 8 June 1843. [GM.NS.20.334]

**KING, THOMAS,** an Irish indentured servant, absconded from Henry Morgan in Baltimore County, Maryland, in June 1747. [MdGaz#102]

**KINLIVEN, MICHAEL,** an indentured servant who emigrated from Limerick to America on the Industry of Westhaven, master James Lowes, in March 1774. [Hook pp, DU]

**KINNAIRD, FRANCIS,** with his wife, three sons and two daughters, from Ireland, landed from the Sally on 19 July 1817, settled in Bastard, Ontario, on 3 October 1817. [PAO.MS154]

**KINNEAR, DAVID,** formerly a Lieutenant of the Royal Artillery, and his two daughters, settled in Bathurst, Ontario, 1 April 1820. [PAO.MS154]

**KIRK, HENRY,** born 1725, an Irish indentured servant, absconded from Benjamin Tasker and Company, Tapasco Iron Works, Baltimore County, Maryland, on 25 June 1745. [MdGaz#13]

**KIRVAN, EDWARD,** from Ireland, settled in Cavan, Ontario, on 9 September 1817. [PAO.MS154]

**KIRVAN, JOHN,** from Ireland, settled in Cavan, Ontario, on 9 September 1817. [PAO.MS154]

**KNOTT, DANIEL,** late of the Royal Sappers, with his wife and 2 daughters, settled in Lanark, Ontario, 1 November 1820. [PAO.MS154]

**KNOWLES, or HURLEY, JOHN,** from Ireland, 5 feet 6 inches, a blacksmith who absconded from Samuel Steven in Talbot County, Maryland, on 12 July 1767. [VaGaz.3.9.1767]

**KOWEN, WILLIAM,** from Ireland, settled in Beckwith, Ontario, on 30 August 1821. [PAO.MS154]

**LACEY, PATRICK,** from Youghal to Maryland on the Encrease of Youghal, master Philip Popplestone, in 1679. [Dorchester Co. Patents, WC#129][MSA.Patents#20/184]

**LACKEY, HUGH,** from Ireland, settled in Huntley, Ontario, on 20 May 1821. [PAO.MS154]

**LACY, MARTIN,** absconded from Joshua Dorsey, Patapsco Ferry, Maryland, 10 September 1750. [MdGaz#283]

**LACY, THOMAS,** from Ireland, settled in Cavan, Newcastle, Ontario, on 3 October 1817. [PAO.MS154]

**LACY, WILLIAM,** a yeoman from Ireland, settled in Cavan, Newcastle, Ontario, on 14 October 1818. [PAO.MS154]

**LADLEY, JAMES,** from Ireland, settled in Goulburn, Ontario, on 2 September 1822. [PAO.MS154]

**LAING, WILLIAM,** a yeoman from Ireland, settled in Smith, Newcastle, Ontario, on 25 November 1818. [PAO.MS154]

**LAIRD, JOHN,** born in Lesk, County Donegal, during 1750, emigrated to USA in 1789, naturalised in Stokes County, North Carolina, on 12 June 1809. [NCSA,CR.090/3111/1]

**LAMB, JOHN,** from Ireland, a former sergeant of the 4th Royal Veterans Battalion, settled in Young, Ontario, on 31 July 1817. [PAO.MS154]

**LAMBSEED, FRANCIS**, from Waterford on the St George of London, to Maryland in 1677.
[SPDom#19/393][MSA.LO.Patents#15/553]

**LANE, DENNIS**, late of the Royal Sappers, with his wife, son and three daughters, settled in Lanark, Ontario, 1 November 1820. [PAO.MS154]

**LANE, JAMES**, from Waterford on the St George of London, to Maryland in 1677.
[SPDom#19/393][MSA.LO.Patents#15/553]

**LANE, MICHAEL,** 5 feet 10 inches, 'recently from Ireland', an indentured servant who absconded from Samuel Canby in Loudoun County, Virginia, on 14 May 1775. [VaGaz.8.6.1775]

**LANE, SUSAN**, from Waterford on the St George of London, to Maryland in 1677.
[SPDom#19/393][MSA.LO.Patents#15/553]

**LANGAM, MARY**, from Waterford on the St George of London, to Maryland in 1677. [SPDom#19/393] [MSA.LO.Patents#15/553]

**LAPKIN, DANIEL,** from Ireland, settled in Cavan, Newcastle, Ontario, on 11 June 1818. [PAO.MS154]

**LARRETT, JAMES,** from Ireland, settled in Huntley, Ontario, on 30 August 1821. [PAO.MS154]

**LATIMER, HUGH,** from Ireland, formerly a sergeant of the Royal Artillery, with his wife, son and daughter, settled in Burgess, Ontario, 26 December 1817. [PAO.MS154]

**LAURIE, ROBERT,** from Ireland, settled in Lanark, Ontario, on 17 September 1821. [PAO.MS154]

**LAWLER, WILLIAM,** from Ireland, a former seaman, settled in Beckwith, Ontario, on 15 September 1817. [PAO.MS154]

**LAWRIE, MATTHEW,** from Ireland, settled in Lanark, Ontario, on 29 October 1821. [PAO.MS154]

**LAWTHER, WILLIAM,** born 1808, son of John Lawther of Cluntagh {1775-1859} and Jane Lawther {1782-1864}, settled in Dubuque Town, USA, died there on 8 November 1866. [Killyleagh g/s, County Down]

**LEAHEY, DENNIS,** an indentured servant who emigrated from Limerick to America on the Industry of Westhaven, master James Lowes, in March 1774. [Hook pp, DU]

**LEAHIE, JOHN,** born 1803, from Conna, County Cork, emigrated from Cove on the Stakesby to Quebec on 8 July 1823, settled in Ramsay township, Ontario. [PAO.prp]

**LEAHY, WILLIAM,** born 1796, with John Leahy born 1798, Mary Leahy born 1801, and William Leahy born 1793, from Mitchelstown, County Cork, emigrated from Cove on the Stakesby to Quebec on 8 July 1823, settled in Ramsay township, Ontario. [PAO.prp]

**LEARY, ALEXANDER,** with his wife, son and two daughters, from Ireland, settled in Ramsay, Ontario, on 10 May 1821. [PAO.MS154]

**LEARY, TIMOTHY,** from Waterford on the St George of London, to Maryland in 1677. [SPDom#19/393][MSA.LO.Patents#15/553]

**LEE, EDWARD,** born 1749, 5 feet 10 inches tall, an Irish indentured servant who absconded from Samuel Arell in Alexandria, Prince George County, Virginia, on 15 December 1776. [VaGaz.27.12.1776]

**LEE, JOHN,** alias George Falmouth, an Irish indentured servant and joiner who absconded from Charles Carter in King George County, Virginia, during 1736. [VaGaz.4.3.1737]

**LEE, JOHN,** from Ireland, a former private of the 2nd Battalion, the 89th Regiment, settled in Bathurst, Ontario, on 9 August 1817. [PAO.MS154]

**LEECH, EDWARD,** from Ireland, settled in Beckwith, Ontario, on 30 October 1822. [PAO.MS154]

**LEECH, ROBERT,** from Ireland, settled in Beckwith, Ontario, on 12 August 1822. [PAO.MS154]

**LEECH, SAMUEL,** from Ireland, settled in Beckwith, Ontario, on 20 August 1820. [PAO.MS154]

**LEGGE, JOHN,** from Youghal to Maryland on the Encrease of Youghal, master Philip Popplestone, in 1679. [Dorchester Co. Patents, WC#129] [MSA.Patents#20/184]

**LEONARD, JAMES,** a former sergeant of the Royal Sappers, with his wife, four sons and three daughters, settled in Lanark, Ontario, 1 November 1820. [PAO.MS154]

**LESLY, WILLIAM,** from Ireland, settled in Lanark, Ontario, on 5 September 1822. [PAO.MS154]

**LESTER, GEORGE,** formerly a conductor of the Commissary Department, with his wife, three sons and four daughters, from Ireland, settled in Bathurst, Ontario, on 1 November 1816, later in Agusta, Ontario, on 31 July 1817. [PAO.MS154]

**LETT, SAMUEL,** from Ireland, settled in Lanark, Ontario, on 17 September 1821. [PAO.MS154]

**LEWIS, ROBERT,** from Ireland, settled in Goulburn, Ontario, on 31 July 1822. [PAO.MS154]

**LEWIS, Mrs....,,** from Antrim, emigrated via Portrush on 27 August 1768 on the Providence, master Thomas Clark, bound for New York, shipwrecked on 8 September, rescued on 19 September by the Friendship of Bo'ness, master James Cowan, bound from Scotland to Charleston, South Carolina. [BNL#3283, 3.2.1769]

**LIDDY, JOHN,** an indentured servant who emigrated from Limerick to America on the Industry of Westhaven, master James Lowes, in March 1774. [Hook pp, DU]

**LINCOLN, GART.,** from Waterford on the St George of London, to Maryland in 1677. [SPDom#19/393][MSA.LO.Patents#15/553]

**LINDSAY, ROBERT,** from Ireland, settled in Goulburn, Ontario, on 20 December 1820. [PAO.MS154]

**LINEY, JOHN,** 6 feet tall, an Irish indentured servant who absconded from Williamsburg, Virginia, during 1751. [VaGaz.8.8.1751]

**LINNEN, PATRICK,** from Ireland, settled in Lanark, Ontario, on 17 September 1821. [PAO.MS154]

**LITTLE, CHRISTOPHER,** a yeoman from Ireland, settled in Cavan, Newcastle, Ontario, on 15 September 1818. [PAO.MS154]

**LIVINGSTON, HUGH,** from Ireland, settled in Dalhousie, Ontario, on 17 September 1821. [PAO.MS154]

**LLOYD, WILLIAM,** born in Ireland, settled in Baltimore, Maryland, in 1771 as a distiller, a Loyalist in 1776, moved to County Westmeath by 1783. [PRO.AO12.6.148]

**LOFTUS, HABIA,** from Youghal to Maryland on the Encrease of Youghal, master Philip Popplestone, in

1679. [Dorchester Co. Patents, WC#129]
[MSA.Patents#20/184]

**LOGAN, MARY,** from Dublin to North Carolina on the
George of Dublin, master Thomas Cumming, in 1735.
[ICJ]

**LOGGAN, EDWARD,** jr., from Ireland, settled in March,
Ontario, on 2 July 1821. [PAO.MS154]

**LOGGAN, FRANCIS,** born 1731, Mary born 1738, John born
1758, and William born 1762, arrived in South Carolina
in January 1768 on the Chichester from Belfast.
[SCCJ.34.1]

**LOMAX, WILLIAM,** from Ireland, settled in Ramsay, Ontario,
on 10 May 1821. [PAO.MS154]

**LONDRY, KATHERINE,** from Youghal to Maryland on the
Encrease of Youghal, master Philip Popplestone, in
1679. [Dorchester Co. Patents, WC#129]
[MSA.Patents#20/184]

**LORD, JAMES,** an indentured servant who absconded from
Richard Welsh, near Patuxent Iron Works, Maryland,
on 29 September 1754. [MdGaz#491]

**LOVE, ROBERT,** settled at Bullock's Creek, South Carolina,
before 1785. [WCA]

**LOVE, WILLIAM,** settled at Bullock's Creek, South Carolina,
before 1785. [WCA]

**LOW, JOHN,** born 1755, a tailor from Donaghadee,
emigrated from Greenock, Scotland, to Philadelphia on
the Magdalene, master James Wallace, in August
1774. [PRO.T47/12]

**LOWEY, ROBERT,** born in 1749, with James Lowey born
1751, emigrated from Belfast on the brigantine
Chichester, master William Reid, arrived in
Charleston, South Carolina, on 25 December 1767.
[SCGaz][SCA]

**LOWREY, MICHAEL,** from Ireland, settled in Huntley,
Ontario, on 31 July 1822. [PAO.MS154]

**LUBY, JOHN,** from Waterford on the St George of London,
to Maryland in 1677.
[SPDom#19/393][MSA.LO.Patents#15/553]

**LUCAS, JOHN,** from Ireland, settled in Beckwith, Ontario, on
30 August 1821. [PAO.MS154]

**LUPTON, EDWARD,** born in Ireland during 1749, a
shoemaker, imprisoned in Williamsburg, Virginia,
during October 1774. [VaGaz.27.10.1774]

**LUPTON, EDWARD,** an indentured servant who emigrated
from Limerick to America on the Industry of
Westhaven, master James Lowes, in March 1774.
[Hook pp, DU]

**LYNCH, MICHAEL,** born 1798, with Julia Lynch born 1801,
from Castletownroche, County Cork, emigrated from
Cove on the Stakesby to Quebec on 8 July 1823,
settled in Pakenham, Ontario. [PAO.prp]

**LYNCH, PATRICK,** emigrated from the Cove of Cork on the
Hebe bound for Quebec on 8 July 1823, settled in
Ramsay township, Ontario. [PAO.prp]

**LYNCH, PHILIP,** from the parish of St Katherine, Jamaica,
late in Westminster, London, probate 9 May 1717
Dublin Register of Deeds

**LYON, DAVID,** emigrated via Portrush on 27 August 1768 on
the Providence, master Thomas Clark, bound for New
York, shipwrecked on 8 September 1768. [BNL#3283,
3.2.1769]

**LYON, JAMES,** emigrated via Portrush on 27 August 1768
on the Providence, master Thomas Clark, bound for
New York, shipwrecked on 8 September 1768.
[BNL#3283, 3.2.1769]

**MACALESTER, ANNE,** born 1757, an indentured servant
who absconded from Richard Somers in Philadelphia
during May 1787. [Phila.Gaz.#258]

**MACAULEY, DENIS,** from Ireland, settled in Cavan,
Newcastle, Ontario, on 8 June 1818. [PAO.MS154]

**MACCLEARY, JOHN,** from Dublin to North Carolina on the
George of Dublin, master Thomas Cumming, in 1735.
[ICJ]

**MACKANDY, JAMES,** a yeoman from Ireland, settled in
Madoc, Midland, Ontario, on 15 October 1818.
[PAO.MS154]

**MACKEMORE, ROBERT,** settled in Lancaster County,
Pennsylvania, before 1734. [LCHS.box#92, fr.2]

**MACKENLEY, THOMAS,** an Irish sailor, absconded from
the Mary, master Alexander Ogilvy, in Chesapeake
Bay off Annapolis on 14 July 1745. [MdGaz#13]

**MACMANUS, MARK,** from Ireland, settled in Brock, Home, Ontario, on 17 July 1817. [PAO.MS154]

**MACNAMARA, THOMAS,** an attorney in Annapolis, Maryland, 1711. [ActsPCCol.1711#1146]

**MCALISTER, MOSES,** a former private of the 104th Regiment, from Ireland, settled in Bathurst, Ontario, on 30 June 1817. [PAO.MS154]

**MCATYER, ANDREW,** emigrated via Portrush on 27 August 1768 on the Providence, master Thomas Clark, bound for New York, shipwrecked on 8 September. [BNL#3283, 3.2.1769]

**MCBRIDE, HARRY,** from Ireland, settled in Huntley, Ontario, on 27 November 1821. [PAO.MS154]

**MCBRIDE, JAMES,** from Ireland, settled in Cavan, Newcastle, Ontario, on 2 May 1818. [PAO.MS154]

**MCCADDEN, HENRY,** formerly a gunner of the King's Artillery, with his wife and son, from Ireland, settled in Drummond, Ontario, on 21 November 1816. [PAO.MS154]

**MCCAFFERY, THOMAS,** a former private of the 70th Regiment, with his wife and daughter, from Ireland, settled in Drummond, Ontario, on 31 March 1817. [PAO.MS154]

**MCCAIN, JAMES,** probably from the parish of Billy, County Antrim, settled in Philadelphia by 1837. [PRONI#D1828/7]

**MCCAIN, ROGER,** an indentured servant who absconded from Nathaniel Chew of the ship Anna, at Lower Marlborough, Maryland, on 24 June 1751. [MdGaz#323]

**MCCAIN, SUSAN,** settled in Chester County, Pennsylvania, before 1730. [CCA.inv#387]

**MCCANN, CHARLES,** an indentured servant who emigrated from Limerick to America on the Industry of Westhaven, master James Lowes, in March 1774. [Hook pp, DU]

**MCCANN, DANIEL,** from Kilmuty Castle, Castle Island, County Kerry, emigrated via Pennsylvania to Carolina in 1783, sought by his cousin Daniel McCann late from Ireland in August 1802. [Raleigh Register:8.8.1802]

**MCCANN, JOHN**, late of the Royal Sappers, with his wife and two sons, settled in Lanark, Ontario, 1 November 1820. [PAO.MS154]

**MCCANNON, ROBERT**, from Ireland, settled in Cavan, Newcastle, Ontario, on 3 February 1818. [PAO.MS154]

**MCCARROLL, SAMUEL**, an indentured servant who emigrated from Belfast on the Bruerton of Liverpool, master John Fowler, to Philadelphia in 1729. [PRONI#D354/71]

**MCCARTER, DUNCAN**, with his wife and two children, emigrated via Portrush on 27 August 1768 on the Providence, master Thomas Clark, bound for New York, shipwrecked on 8 September. [BNL#3283, 3.2.1769]

**MCCARTHY, CHARLES**, born 1796, from Rathkeal, County Limerick, emigrated from Cove on the Stakesby to Quebec on 8 July 1823, settled in Ramsay township, Ontario. [PAO.prp]

**MCCARTHY, DANIEL,** from Ireland, a former sergeant of the 97th Regiment, settled in Wogord, Ontario, on 31 July 1817, and in Kittley, Ontario, on 22 May 1818. [PAO.MS154]

**MCCARTHY, DENIS,** an Irish indentured servant of Benjamin Backhouse a tavernkeeper in South Carolina, 1767. [see B. Backhouse, probate, 1767, South Carolina]

**MCCARTHY, OWEN**, and his wife, settled in Beckwith, Ontario, on 4 December 1821. [PAO.MS154]

**MCCARTHY, WILLIAM,** from Ireland, a former private of the 97th Regiment, settled in Beckwithwith, Ontario, 23 July 1818. [PAO.MS154]

**MCCARTNEY, NICHOLAS,** born 1747, 5 feet 9 inches tall, a shoemaker and indentured servant from Ireland who absconded from Zachariah Hendrick in Cumberland County, Virginia, on 9 December 1773. [VaGaz.17.2.1774]

**MCCARTY, LAWRENCE,** absconded from Joshua Dorsey, Patapsco Ferry, Maryland, on 10 September 1750. [MdGaz#283]

**MCCAULEY, CHARLES**, from Ireland, settled in Cavan,
Newcastle, Ontario, on 9 September 1817.
[PAO.MS154]

**MCCAULEY, DANIEL**, from Ireland, settled in Cavan,
Newcastle, Ontario, on September 1817. [PAO.MS154]

**MCCAULEY, FLORENCE**, from Ireland, settled in Cavan,
Newcastle, Ontario, on 9 September 1817.
[PAO.MS154]

**MCCAULEY, JOHN,** from Ireland, settled in Cavan,
Newcastle, Ontario, on 9 September 1817.
[PAO.MS154]

**MCCAY, JAMES LEWIS,** emigrated via Portrush on 27
August 1768 on the Providence, master Thomas Clark,
bound for New York, shipwrecked on 8 September.
[BNL#3283, 3.2.1769]

**MCCLANAHAN, ROBERT,** an indentured servant who
emigrated from Belfast on the Bruerton of Liverpool,
master John Fowler, to Philadelphia in 1729.
[PRONI#D354/71]

**MCCLEAN, JAMES,** arrived in South Carolina in January
1768 on the brigantine Chichester, master William
Reid, from Belfast. [SCCJ.34.1]

**MCCOLLUM, MATTHEW,** settled in Shelbourne, Ontario, on
4 April 1821. [PAO.MS154]

**MCCONNELL, ALEXANDER**, settled in Chester County,
Pennsylvania, before 1729. [CCA.inv#348]

**MCCONNELL, ALEXANDER,** a yeoman from Ireland,
settled in Smith, Newcastle, Ontario, on 9 November
1818. [PAO.MS154]

**MCCONNELL, MICHAEL,** late of the York Chasseurs, with
his wife, son and daughter, land grant in Bathurst,
Ontario, 22 September 1819. [PAO.MS154]

**MCCORD, THOMAS,** from Ireland, settled in Huntley,
Ontario, on 30 July 1821. [PAO.MS154]

**MCCORMACK, JAMES,** born in County Cavan, on 6 August
1751, settled in New Windsor, New York, died in
Newburgh, New York, on 11 November 1865.
[GM.NS.3.1.283]

**MCCORMICK, JAMES,** a teacher from Ireland, settled in
Smith, Newcastle, Ontario, on 21 November 1818.
[PAO.MS154]

**MCCORMICK, WILLIAM,** a yeoman from Ireland, settled in Smith, Newcastle, Ontario, on 2 November 1818. [PAO.MS154]

**MCCOUCHEY, THOMAS,** from Ireland, settled in Huntley, Ontario, on 14 August 1822. [PAO.MS154]

**MCCOURT, THOMAS,** late of the Royal Sappers, with his wife, four sons and two daughters, settled in Lanark, Ontario, 1 November 1820. [PAO.MS154]

**MCCRACHEN, ARTHUR,** born 1727, Ruth born 1729, Mary born 1750, Jane born 1751, William born 1753, Thomas born 1754, Margaret born 1756, James born 1757, Arthur born 1758, Samuel born 1760, Ruth born 1762, John born 1764, and James born 1766, arrived in South Carolina in January 1768 on the brigantine Chichester, master William Reid, from Belfast. [SCCJ.34.1]

**MACCRAKAN, ROBERT,** and his wife Esther, from Dublin to North Carolina on the George of Dublin, master Thomas Cumming, in 1735. [ICJ]

**MCCRUDEN, MORRIS,** from Ireland, settled in Dalhousie, Ontario, on 24 January 1822. [PAO.MS154]

**MCCULLOCH, JOHN,** with his wife, 2 sons and a daughter, land grant in Burgess, Ontario, 16 June 1819. [PAO.MS154]

**MCCULLY, JOHN,** an indentured servant who emigrated from Belfast on the Bruerton of Liverpool, master John Fowler, to Philadelphia in 1729. [PRONI#D354/71]

**MCDANIEL, ANNE,** born in Dublin around 1718, settled in Maryland about 1742, sought in 1753. [MdGaz#435]

**MCDERMOT, PATRICK,** with his wife, two sons and one daughter, from Ireland, settled in Ramsay, Ontario, on 10 May 1821. [PAO.MS154]

**MCDONALD, JAMES,** born in Ireland around 1754, a laborer, a felon imprisoned in Williamsburg, Virginia, in October 1774. [VaGaz.27.10.1774]

**MCDONALD, JAMES,** an indentured servant who emigrated from Limerick to America on the Industry of Westhaven, master James Lowes, in March 1774. [Hook pp, DU]

**MCDONALD, JOHN**, a former corporal of the York Chasseurs, settled in Bathurst, Ontario, on 22 September 1819. [PAO.MS154]

**MCDONELL, COLIN,** a weaver from Ireland, settled in Smith, Newcastle, Ontario, on 19 January 1819. [PAO.MS154]

**MCDONELL, JAMES,** from Ireland, late a sergeant of the 99th Regiment, with his wife and daughter, settled in Sherbrooke, Ontario, on 24 June 1822. [PAO.MS154]

**MCDONNELL, JAMES**, with his wife and two daughters, arrived on the Thomas 7 August 1819, settled in Bathurst, Ontario, 15 April 1820. [PAO.MS154]

**MCDONNELL, JOHN,** a Quaker, with his wife Betty, from Dungannon, County Tyrone, settled in Wilmington, North Carolina, by June 1771. [PRONI#D1044/294]

**MCDONNELL, PATRICK**, and his wife, arrived on the Thomas 7 August 1819, settled in Bathurst, Ontario, 15 April 1820. [PRO.MS154]

**MCDOOE, HUGH,** an indentured servant who emigrated from Belfast on the Bruerton of Liverpool, master John Fowler, to Philadelphia in 1729. [PRONI#D354/71]

**MCDOWAL, WILLIAM,** from Ireland, settled in Goulburn, Ontario, on 2 November 1822. [PAO.MS154]

**MCENTEE, ELEANOR,** born 1744 in County Monaghan, widow of Thomas Hanna, settled in USA during 1808, died in New York on 18 December 1856. [GM.NS2.2.368]

**MCENTIRE, Mrs NANCY,** born in Ireland during 1748, settled in Burke County, North Carolina, during 1788, died in Morgantown 12 June 1830. [North Carolina Spectator, 18.6.1830]

**MCEVOY, DANIEL,** sr., from Ireland, settled in Huntley, Ontario, on 31 July 1822. [PAO.MS154]

**MCEVOY, DARBY,** jr, from Ireland, settled in Huntley, Ontario, on 11 September 1822. [PAO.MS154]

**MCEVOY, MATTHEW,** from Ireland, settled in Huntley, Ontario, on 16 September 1821. [PAO.MS154]

**MCEVOYE, JOHN,** from Ireland, settled in Huntley, Ontario, on 11 September 1822. [PAO.MS154]

**MCEWAN, THOMAS,** a former sergeant of the 6th Regiment, from Ireland, settled in Montague, Ontario, on 30 July 1817. [PAO.MS154]

**MCFADDEN, JAMES,** a former gunner of the Royal Artillery, with his wife, from Ireland, settled in Edwardsburgh, Ontario, on 30 June 1817. [PAO.MS154]

**MCFADDIN, JOHN,** emigrated via Portrush on 27 August 1768 on the Providence, master Thomas Clark, bound for New York, shipwrecked on 8 September. [BNL#3283, 3.2.1769]

**MCFARLIN, JOHN,** born 1758, and Mary born 1760, arrived in South Carolina in January 1768 on the brigantine Chichester, master William Reid, from Belfast. [SCCJ.34.1]

**MCFARRAN, .....,** son of James McFarran, from Ireland to North Carolina in 1734. [ICJ]

**MCGANN, JOHN,** formerly a private of the Glengarry Fencibles, from Ireland, settled in Drummond, Ontario, on 16 July 1816. [PAO.MS154]

**MCGAURIN, MICHAEL,** from Liscarros, County Cork, emigrated from the Cove of Cork on the Hebe bound for Quebec on 8 July 1823, settled in Ramsay township, Ontario. [PAO.prp]

**MCGEE, ARCHIBALD,** from Ireland, settled in Goulburn, Ontario, on 23 August 1820. [PAO.MS154]

**MCGEE, JAMES,** from Ireland, settled in Lanark, Ontario, on 17 September 1821. [PAO.MS154]

**MCGEE, JOHN,** with his wife and three daughters, from Ireland, settled in Lanark, Ontario, on 1 October 1821. [PAO.MS154]

**MCGEE, THOMAS D'ARCY,** born in Carlingford during 1823, died in Ottawa during 1868. [GM.NSN3N5N690]

**MCGEE, WILLIAM,** from Ireland, settled in Lanark, Ontario, on 17 September 1821. [PAO.MS154]

**MCGEE, WILLIAM,** from Ireland, settled in Goulburn, Ontario, on 30 October 1822. [PAO.MS154]

**MCGILL, ROWLAND,** born in Ireland, 5 feet 5 inches tall, well set, fair complexion, formerly of the Maryland Forces, deserted from the 44th Regiment of Foot in Maryland in January 1759. [Md Gaz#715]

**MCGINNIS, DANIEL,** 5 feet 7 inches tall, a schoolmaster from Ireland, sought by Andrew Meek in Augusta County, Virginia, in August 1774. [VaGaz.4.8.1774]

**MCGINNIS, HUGH,** with his wife and two sons, from Ireland, landed from the Eclipse on 8 August 1817, settled in Landsdowne, Ontario, on 30 September 1817. [PAO.MS154]

**MCGINNIS, JOHN,** formerly a sergeant of the Glengarry Fencibles, with his wife and two sons, from Ireland, settled in Drummond, Ontario, on 16 July 1816. [PAO.MS154]

**MCGINNIS, WILLIAM,** formerly a private of the Glengarry Fencibles, from Ireland, settled in Drummond, Ontario, on 16 July 1816. [PAO.MS154]

**MCGIVERN, JOHN,** from Ireland, settled in Goulburn, Ontario, on 12 August 1822. [PAO.MS154]

**MCGOUN, JAMES,** an indentured servant who absconded from John Smyth, Queen Anne County, Maryland, in September 1754. [MdGaz#492]

**MCGRORY, DAVID,** from Ireland, settled in Westminster, London, Ontario, on 22 May 1818. [PAO.MS154]

**MCGUFFIE, JAMES,** from Ireland, settled in Westminster, London, Ontario, on 10 October 1817. [PAO.MS154]

**MCGUIER, THOMAS,** born 1732, an Irish indentured servant and joiner who arrived in America during 1745, absconded from Norfolk, Virginia, on 5 January 1752. [VaGaz.10.1.1752]

**MCGUIGAN, JOHN,** late of the Royal Sappers, with his wife, son and daughter, settled in Lanark, Ontario, 1 November 1820. [PAO.MS154]

**MCGUILAND, ARCHIBALD,** from Ireland, settled in Lanark, Ontario, on 23 August 1821. [PAO.MS154]

**MCGUILL, JOHN,** from Ireland, settled in Cavan, Newcastle, Ontario, on 19 March 1818. [PAO.MS154]

**MCGUIRE, JAMES,** son of Philip McGuire, settled in New York by 1845. [Killyleagh g/s, County Down]

**MCGUIRE, JOHN,** formerly a private of the 17th Light Dragoons, with his wife, from Ireland, settled in Drummond, Ontario, on 17 October 1816. [PAO.MS154]

**MCGUIRE, LAWRENCE,** from Ireland, settled in Cavan, Newcastle, Ontario, on 23 April 1818. [PAO.MS154]

**MCGUIRE, PATRICK,** from Ireland, settled in Cavan, Newcastle, Ontario, on 17 April 1818. [PAO.MS154]

**MCHENRY, JOHN,** emigrated via Portrush on 27 August 1768 on the <u>Providence</u>, master Thomas Clark, bound for New York, shipwrecked on 8 September. [BNL#3283, 3.2.1769]

**MCHEWAN, ROBERT,** from Ireland, formerly of the 4th Royal Veterans, with his wife, son and three daughters, settled in Drummond, Ontario, on 25 September 1817, and in Elmsby, Ontario, on 27 February 1818. [PAO.MS154]

**MCILROY, DAVID,** from Ireland, settled in Westminster, London, Ontario, on 14 April 1818. [PAO.MS154]

**MCINSTARY, JAMES,** from Ireland, settled in Marlborough, Ontario, on 9 September 1822. [PAO.MS154]

**MCKAY, JOHN,** from Ireland, settled in Lanark, Ontario, on 20 March 1821. [PAO.MS154]

**MCKEAN, JAMES,** a former private of the Glengarry Regiment, with his wife and son, from Ireland, settled in Drummond, Ontario, on 16 July 1816. [PAO.MS154]

**MCKENNA, WILLIAM,** a yeoman from Ireland, settled in Smith, Newcastle, Ontario, on 24 November 1818. [PAO.MS154]

**MACKENZIE, PATRICK,** born in Ireland 1726, a convict indentured servant, who absconded from Benjamin Ryan, in July 1746. [MdGaz#66]

**MCKENZIE, ROBERT SHELTON,** born at Drew's Court, County Limerick, on 22 June 1809, graduated LL.D. from Glasgow University in 1834, a schoolmaster at Fermoy, County Cork, a journalist in England, a litterateur in New York and Philadelphia, died in Philadelphia on 30 November 1880. [RGG#386]

**MCKETRICK, MICHAEL,** late of the Royal Sappers, with his wife, son and 2 daughters, settled in Lanark, Ontario, 1 November 1820. [PAO.MS154]

**MCKEWAN, JOHN,** from Ireland, settled in Beck, Ontario, on 2 July 1821. [PAO.MS154]

**MCKIBBEY, WALTER,** a yeoman from Ireland, settled in Smith, Newcastle, Ontario, on 27 February 1819. [PAO.MS154]

**MCKINNEY, ALEXANDER,** with his wife, son and two daughters, from Ireland, landed from the <u>Ocean</u> on 22 July 1817, settled in Landsdowne, Ontario, on 4 October 1817. [PAO.MS154]

**MCKINNEY, .........,,** probably from the parish of Billy in County Antrim, settled in Philadelphia by 1837. [PRONI#D1828/7]

**MCLATCHIE, HUGH,** from Ireland, settled in Lanark, Ontario, on 24 September 1821. [PAO.MS154]

**MCLATCHIE, WILLIAM,** from Ireland, settled in Lanark, Ontario, on 24 September 1821. [PAO.MS154]

**MCLAUGHLAN, WILLIAM,** a yeoman from Ireland, settled in Cavan, Newcastle, Ontario, on 15 September 1818. [PAO.MS154]

**MCLAUGHLIN, FERGUS,** an indentured servant from Ireland on the <u>Providence of Ireland,</u>160 tons, master John Hamilton, arrived in Middlesex County on the Rappahannock River, Virginia, on 30 March 1699. [XJVa.I.458]

**MCLEAN, JAMES,** born in 1748, emigrated from Belfast on the brigantine <u>Chichester</u>, master William Reid, arrived in Charleston, South Carolina, on 25 December 1767. [SCGaz][SCA]

**MCLEAN, JAMES,** formerly a sergeant of the Glengarry Fencibles, from Ireland, settled in Burgess, Ontario, on 25 September 1816. [PAO.MS154]

**MCLEAN, JAMES,** from Ireland, a former army sergeant, settled in Wolford, Ontario, 18 May 1818. [PAO.MS154]

**MCLELLAND, HUGH,** landed from the <u>Richard and John</u> in 1819, settled in Shelbourne, Ontario, on 30 March 1821. [PAO.MS154]

**MCLELLAND, JOHN,** with his wife, three sons and a daughter, landed from the <u>Ocean</u> on 22 July 1817, settled in Landsdowne, Ontario, on 3 October 1817. [PAO.MS154]

**MCLELLAND, SAMUEL,** landed from the Richard and John in 1819, settled in Shelbourne, Ontario, on 30 March 1821. [PAO.MS154]

**MCMAHON, DANIEL,** an indentured servant who emigrated from Limerick to America on the Industry of Westhaven, master James Lowes, in March 1774. [Hook pp, DU]

**MCMAHONY, EDMUND,** from Waterford on the St George of London, to Maryland in 1677. [SPDom#19/393][MSA.LO.Patents#15/553]

**MCMANUS, EDWARD,** with his wife, from Ireland, settled in Ramsay, Ontario, on 2 April 1821. [PAO.MS154]

**MCMANUS, JOHN,** with his wife and son, from Ireland, settled in Lanark, Ontario, on 26 September 1821. [PAO.MS154]

**MCMULLEN, ALEXANDER,** from Dublin, probate 9 June 1766, New York.

**MCNALLEY, ANDREW,** from Ireland, settled in Goulburn, Ontario, on 30 October 1822. [PAO.MS154]

**MCNALLEY, MATTHEW,** from Ireland, settled in Beckwith, Ontario, on 30 January 1820. [PAO.MS154]

**MCNAMARA, CATHERINE,** an indentured servant who emigrated from Limerick to America on the Industry of Westhaven, master James Lowes, in March 1774. [Hook pp, DU]

**MCNAMARA, PATRICK,** a former private of the Glengarry Regiment, with his wife, two sons and a daughter, from Ireland, settled in Drummond, Ontario, on 16 July 1816. [PAO.MS154]

**MCNAMEE, PATRICK,** formerly a private of the Glengarry Fencibles, with his wife and daughter, from Ireland, settled in Burgess, Ontario, on 1 November 1816. [PAO.MS154]

**MCNEIL, HUGH,** emigrated from Ireland to America in 1763, settled in Bedford, Pennsylvania, Loyalist soldier, moved to Burton, New Brunswick. [PRO.AO12.40.262]

**MCNEIL, JOHN,** from Ireland, settled in Dalhousie, Ontario, on 24 September 1821. [PAO.MS154]

**MCNEIL, NEIL,** with his wife, two sons and family, from Ireland, settled in Dalhousie, Ontario, on 24 September 1821. [PAO.MS154]

**MCNEILEY, BRICE,** from Ireland, settled in Beckwith, Ontario, on 12 July 1822. [PAO.MS154]

**MCNEILEY, JAMES,** from Ireland, settled in Beckwith, Ontario, on 12 July 1822. [PAO.MS154]

**MCNEILEY, JOHN,** from Ireland, settled in Beckwith, Ontario, on 26 November 1822. [PAO.MS154]

**MCNEILL, ARCHIBALD,** a yeoman from Ireland, settled in Smith, Newcastle, Ontario, on 22 February 1819. [PAO.MS154]

**MCNICE, JAMES,** from Ireland, a former sergeant of the Glengarry Fencibles, settled in Oxford, Ontario, on 31 July 1817. [PAO.MS154]

**MCPEAK, JOHN,** from Ireland, settled in Brock, Home, Ontario, on 11 Octoer 1817. [PAO.MS154]

**MCRORY,** or **GREGORY, JAMES,** a vagrant imprisoned in Dundalk, was to be transported to the colonies in 1718. [NLI.ms11949]

**MCVICKAR, ARCHIBALD,** from County Antrim, a merchant in New York, probate 10 May 1779 New York

**MACKIE, JOHN,** an Irish indentured servant and blacksmith who absconded from William Aylett in Westmoreland County, Virginia, on 8 July 1739. [VaGaz.10.8.1739]

**MACOUN, THOMAS,** an Irish indentured servant who absconded from St Mary's County, on the Potomac River, Maryland, on 5 August 1739. [VaGaz.10.8.1739]

**MADDIN, CORNELIUS,** an Irish indentured servant who absconded from Robert Dudley in King and Queen County, Virginia, in 1739. [VaGaz.2.2.1739]

**MADDIN, THOMAS,** an indentured servant who emigrated from Limerick to America on the Industry of Westhaven, master James Lowes, in March 1774. [Hook pp, DU]

**MADDEN, THOMAS,** born 1785, with wife Ellen born 1791, and children Jeremiah born 1807, Mary born 1814, John born 1816, and Thomas born 1818, from Cork, emigrated from Cove on the Stakesby to Quebec on 8 July 1823, settled in Ramsay township, Ontario. [PAO.prp]

**MADELL, BENJAMIN,** a yeoman from Ireland, settled in Esquiday, Newcastle, Ontario, on 10 October 1818. [PAO.MS154]

**MAGEE, SAMUEL,** from Ireland, graduated CM from Glasgow University in 1833, *'obliged to leave this country for America on1st April next' {University Minutes, 22 March 1833}*[RGG#415]

**MAGELTON, ANDREW,** born 1712, Elizabeth born 1717, Vance born 1750, Peter born 1754, and James born 1757, arrived in South Carolina in January 1768 on the brigantine <u>Chichester,</u> master William Reid, from Belfast. [SCCJ.34.1]

**MAGRATH, CATHER,** and young daughter, from Youghal to Maryland on the <u>Encrease of Youghal</u>, master Philip Popplestone, in 1679. [Dorchester Co. Patents, WC#129] [MSA.Patents#20/184]

**MAGRATH, MORGAN,** from Youghal to Maryland on the <u>Encrease of Youghal</u>, master Philip Popplestone, in 1679. [Dorchester Co. Patents, WC#129] [MSA.Patents#20/184]

**MAHAFFY, MARTIN,** born 1728, Martha, born 1741, and Mary born 1763, emigrated from Belfast on the <u>Chichester</u>, William Reed, to South Carolina, arrived in January 1768. [SCCJ.IV.1]

**MAHARRY, HUGH,** a farmer from Ireland, settled in Cavan, Newcastle, Ontario, on 11 September 1818. [PAO.MS154]

**MAHONEY, DARBY,** an indentured servant who absconded from Charles Ridgely, Baltimore County, Maryland, on 8 July 1753. [MdGaz#431]

**MAHONY, HENRY,** born 1797, with Bridget Mahony born 1793, from Mallow, County Cork, emigrated from Cove on the <u>Stakesby</u> to Quebec on 8 July 1823, settled in Pakenham, Ontario. [PAO.prp]

**MAKKY, JOHN,** born in County Down during 1800, died in Charleston, South Carolina, on 10 April 1844, buried in the Old Scots Church there. [Charleston g/s]

**MALCOLMSON, JAMES,** born in Ireland during 1768, a minister in Williamsburgh, died 25 September 1804, buried in the Old Scots Church of Charleston, South Carolina. [Charleston g/s]

**MALCOLMSON, ROBERT,** from Ireland, settled in Goulburn, Ontario, on 30 August 1821. [PAO.MS154]

**MALIGEE, DANIEL,** an Irish indentured servant in Barbados, 1656. [Minutes of the Council of Barbados, 8/1656]

**MALLARD, JOSEPH,** from Ireland, late a sergeant of the 70th Regiment, with his wife, two sons and two daughters, settled in Bathurst, Ontario, on 25 March 1821. [PAO.MS154]

**MALLET, JAMES,** an indentured servant who emigrated from Belfast on the Bruerton of Liverpool, master John Fowler, to Philadelphia in 1729. [PRONI#D354/71]

**MALONE, BRIDGET,** an indentured servant who emigrated from Limerick to America on the Industry of Westhaven, master James Lowes, in March 1774. [Hook pp, DU]

**MALONE, JEREMIAH,** an indentured servant who emigrated from Limerick to America on the Industry of Westhaven, master James Lowes, in March 1774. [Hook pp, DU]

**MALONEY, JAMES,** from Ireland, settled in Lanark, Ontario, on 26 September 1821. [PAO.MS154]

**MANARY, JOHN,** born 1745, arrived in South Carolina in January 1768 on the brigantine Chichester, master William Reid, from Belfast. [SCCJ.34.1]

**MANION, THOMAS,** with his wife, two sons and a daughter, from Ireland, settled in Bathurst, Ontario, on 15 June 1816. [PAO.MS154]

**MANTETT, ROBERT,** a sailor, ran away from the Frisby, master John Knill, off Annapolis 30 June 1753. [MdGaz#427]

**MANTLE, JOHN,** born 1778, his wife Ellen born 1783, and children James born 1805, Mary born 1807, Ellen born 1811, Margaret born 1813, Robert born 1817 and Katherine born 1821, from Rathcormick, County Cork, emigrated from Cove on the Stakesby to Quebec on 8 July 1823, settled in Huntley, Ontario. [PAO.prp]

**MARA, JOHN,** born 1781, with his wife Joanna born 1787, and children Mary born 1808, John born 1811, Joanna born 1815, Bridget born 1817, Thomas born 1818, and Ellen born 1820, from Rathcormick, County Cork, emigrated from Cove on the Stakesby to Quebec on 8 July 1823, settled in Ramsay township, Ontario. [PAO.prp]

**MARA, RICHARD,** from Ireland, settled in Huntley, Ontario, on 16 September 1821. [PAO.MS154]

**MARR, WILLIAM,** born 1707, an Irish indentured servant who absconded from Charles Chiswell in Hanover County, Virginia, during January 1737. [VaGaz.18.2.1737]

**MARRAN, DAVID,** settled in St George's parish, Georgia, before 1776, a Loyalist soldier, moved to Larne, Ireland, by 1785. [PRO.AO12.3.101]

**MARSHALL, MARY,** an Irish indentured servant who absconded from John Chiswell in Hanover County, Virginia, in 1751. [VaGaz.17.10.1751]

**MARSHALL, SAMUEL,** son of Mary Marshall {1814-1879}, settled in USA. [Kilcairn g/s]

**MARTIN, CHRISTOPHER,** 5 feet 10 inches tall, a runaway Irish indentured servant who was imprisoned in Frederick County, Virginia, during August 1751. [VaGaz.17.10.1751]

**MARTIN, CORNELIUS,** an indentured servant who emigrated from Limerick to America on the Industry of Westhaven, master James Lowes, in March 1774. [Hook pp, DU]

**MARTIN, FINIAN,** a free person, arrived in Barbados from Ireland during 1654. [Minutes of the Council of Barbados, 6.12.1654]

**MARTIN, HENRY,** from Ireland, settled in Lanark, Ontario, on 17 September 1821. [PAO.MS154]

**MARTIN, PATRICK,** from Ireland, settled in Huntley, Ontario, on 30 May 1822. [PAO.MS154]

**MARTIN, SAMUEL,** a merchant in Antigua, 1757. [BL.Add.MS.41349/50]

**MARTIN, THOMAS,** 5 feet 10 inches tall, an Irish indentured servant who absconded from the snow Industrious Bee at Sandy Point, Virginia, on 1 June 1752. [VaGaz.5.5.1751]

**MASCALL, JANE,** from Waterford on the St George of London, to Maryland in 1677. [SPDom#19/393][MSA.LO.Patents#15/553]

**MATHESON, ALEXANDER,** a former quartermaster sergeant of the Glengarry Fencibles, from Ireland,

settled in Kitley, Ontario, on 26 June 1817.
[PAO.MS154]

**MATTHEWS, DANIEL,** a tailor from Ireland, settled in Smith, Newcastle, Ontario, on 3 March 1819. [PAO.MS154]

**MATTHEWS, JUDE,** born 1714, an Irish indentured servant who absconded from Coleman Read in Westmoreland County, Virginia, on 17 June 1739. [VaGaz.18.8.1739]

**MATTHEWSON, DONALD,** from Ireland, settled in Marlborough, Ontario, on 31 July 1822. [PAO.MS154]

**MAXWELL, ROBERT,** from Ireland, settled in March, Ontario, on 7 September 1822. [PAO.MS154]

**MAY, JOHN,** an indentured servant who emigrated from Limerick to America on the Industry of Westhaven, master James Lowes, in March 1774. [Hook pp, DU]

**MAY, JOHN,** a gardener from Ireland, settled in Smith, Newcastle, Ontario, on 19 January 1819. [PAO.MS154]

**MAYES, JAMES,** settled in Lancaster County, Pennsylvania, died 1734. [LCHS, box#92, fr1]

**MAYNERS, ANDREW,** from Ireland, settled in Cavan, Newcastle, Ontario, on 15 September 1818.
[PAO.MS154]

**MEAD, MICHAEL,** from Ireland, late of the 1st Royal Regiment, with his wife and son, settled in Lanark, Ontario, on 8 November 1820. [PAO.MS154]

**MEADE, MICHAEL,** from Ireland, a former corporal of the 1st Royal Veteran Battalion, with his wife, son and daughter, settled in Burgess, Ontario, on 22 October 1817. [PAO.MS154]

**MEAGHER, DAVID,** from Ireland, settled in Huntley, Ontario, on 24 August 1822. [PAO.MS154]

**MEAHER, RICHARD,** from Waterford on the St George of London, to Maryland in 1677.
[SPDom#19/393][MSA.LO.Patents#15/553]

**MEAHER, T.,** from Waterford on the St George of London, to Maryland in 1677.
[SPDom#19/393][MSA.LO.Patents#15/553]

**MEARS, JOHN,** from Ireland, settled in Goulburn, Ontario, on 10 August 1821. [PAO.MS154]

**MELY, PATRICK,** from Waterford on the St George of London, to Maryland in 1677.
[SPDom#19/393][MSA.LO.Patents#15/553]

**MERRITT, ADAM,** from Youghal to Maryland on the
Encrease of Youghal, master Philip Popplestone, in
1679. [Dorchester Co. Patents, WC#129]
[MSA.Patents#20/184]

**MERRY, PETER,** from Waterford on the St George of
London, to Maryland in 1677.
[SPDom#19/393][MSA.LO.Patents#15/553]

**MEYNER, JOHN,** a yeoman from Ireland, settled in Cavan,
Newcastle, Ontario, on 27 October 1818.
[PAO.MS154]

**MILFORD, SAMUEL,** from Ireland, settled in Marsh, Ontario,
on 10 January 1821. [PAO.MS154]

**MILHOUSE, ROBERT,** agent for Arthur Dobbs in
Carrickfergus, County Antrim, emigrated from Dublin to
Brunswick, North Carolina, in 1751. [PRONI#D162/52]

**MILLANE, JEREMIAH,** with Joanna, from Ballybibblin,
County Cork, emigrated from the Cove of Cork on the
Hebe bound for Quebec on 8 July 1823, settled in
Ramsay township, Ontario. [PAO.prp]

**MILLBY, alias WILLOUGHBY, ROBERT,** a weaver and
former dragoon of Lord Stair's Regiment, absconded
from Lawrence Washington 16 August 1748.
[MdGaz#174]

**MILLER, JAMES,** from Ireland, a former sergeant of the 5th
Dragoon Guards, settled in Bathurst, Ontario, on 9
August 1817. [PAO.MS154]

**MILLER, Miss .....,** in Meikle Dunragit, Ireland, 1771, then in
Philadelphia. [NAS.GD135.1649]

**MILLIKEN, JOHN,** born in 1849, son of Samuel Milliken
{1821-1856}, died in Philadelphia on 27 June 1854.
[Killyreagh g/s, County Down]

**MILLS, ROBERT,** born 1752, arrived from Ireland in
September 1774, a gardener and indentured servant
who absconded from Samuel Hanson in Charles
County, Maryland, in 1774. [VaGaz.24.11.1774]

**MIUNHANE, JOHN,** from Youghal to Maryland on the
Encrease of Youghal, master Philip Popplestone, in
1679. [Dorchester Co. Patents,
WC#129][MSA.Patents#20/184]

**MONTGOMERY, HENRY,** from Ireland, settled in Lanark,
Ontario, on 15 October 1821. [PAO.MS154]

**MONTGOMERY, JOHN,** from Ireland, settled in Goulburn, Ontario, on 1 March 1822. [PAO.MS154]

**MONTGOMERY, L.,** a yeoman from Ireland, settled in Cavan, Newcastle, Ontario, on 22 August 1818. [PAO.MS154]

**MONTGOMERY, ROBERT,** from Ireland, settled in Goulburn, Ontario, on 10 September 1821. [PAO.MS154]

**MONTGOMERY. WILLIAM,** from Ireland, settled in Huntley, Ontario, on 16 October 1820. [PAO.MS154]

**MOONEY, DANIEL,** from Ireland, settled in Cavan, Newcastle, Ontario, on 19 March 1818. [PAO.MS154]

**MOONEY, DANIEL,** from Ireland, settled in Beckwith, Ontario, on 25 January 1820. [PAO.MS154]

**MOONEY, WILLIAM,** from Ireland, settled in Huntley, Ontario, on 29 October 1820. [PAO.MS154]

**MOOR, ANDREW,** born 1750, emigrated from Belfast on the Chichester, William Reed, to South Carolina, arrived in January 1768. [SCCJ.IV.1]

**MOOR, ISRAEL,** born 1712, Nancy born 1717, William born 1740, Israel born 1743, Elizabeth born 1747, Richard born 1749, Jane born 1751, Christopher born 1753, Ann born 1755, and Elinor born 1762, arrived in South Carolina in January 1768 on the brigantine Chichester, master William Reed, from Belfast. [SCCJ.34.1]

**MOOR, ROWLAND,** an indentured servant who emigrated from Belfast on the Bruerton of Liverpool, master John Fowler, to Philadelphia in 1729. [PRONI#D354/71]

**MOORE, JAMES,** an Irish indentured servant who absconded from John Schooler in Caroline County, Virginia, on 27 December 1739. [VaGaz.25.1.1740]

**MOORE, JAMES,** Donegal Place, Belfast, married Lydia, daughter of Archibald Montgomery of New Orleans, there on 3 April 1877. [S#10,520]

**MOORE, JOHN,** a laborer from Ireland, settled in Cavan, Newcastle, Ontario, on 25 September 1818. [PAO.MS154]

**MOORE, ROBERT,** a former sergeant of the 104th Regiment, from Ireland, settled in Bathurst, Ontario, on 30 June 1817. [PAO.MS154]

**MOORE, ROBERT,** a yeoman from Ireland, settled in
Toronto, Home, Ontario, on 22 April 1819.
[PAO.MS154]

**MOORE, THOMAS,** from Ireland, settled in Marlborough,
Ontario, on 14 August 1822. [PAO.MS154]

**MOORE, WILLIAM,** formerly a driver of the Royal Artillery,
with his wife and son, from Ireland, settled in
Drummond, Ontario, on 26 October 1816.
[PAO.MS154]

**MOORE, WILLIAM GAMBLE,** a cutler, settled in
Philadelphia by 1793. [PRONI#T3525]

**MOORHEAD, JAMES,** born 1709, Jane born 1710, Rose
born 1743, James born 1750, Prudence born 1754,
and James born 1762, arrived in South Carolina in
January 1768 on the brigantine Chichester, master
William Reid, from Belfast. [SCCJ.34.1]

**MOORHEAD, JOHN,** from Ireland, settled in Huntley,
Ontario, on 25 October 1822. [PAO.MS154]

**MOORHEAD, SAMUEL,** from Ireland, settled in Huntley,
Ontario, on 29 November 1821. [PAO.MS154]

**MOORHEAD, SAMUEL,** jr., from Ireland, settled in Huntley,
Ontario, on 30 October 1822. [PAO.MS154]

**MOORHEAD, STEPHENSON,** from Ireland, settled in
Huntley, Ontario, on 29 November 1821. [PAO.MS154]

**MOORHOUSE, THOMAS,** from Ireland, settled in Beckwith,
Ontario, on 20 August 1820. [PAO.MS154]

**MORAN, THOMAS J.,** educated at Trinity College, Dublin, a
schoolmaster in Washington, North Carolina, in 1826,
died in Tuscumbia, Alabama, on 19 May 1827.
[Washington Herald, 24.7.1827]

**MOREIN, JOHN,** born in Ireland around 1724, 5 feet 9
inches tall, red hair, arrived on the snow Tryal, Captain
Freebairn, absconded from John Smith Prather,
Bladensburg, Virginia, in August 1759.
[MdGaz#746][MdGaz774]

**MOREN, GEORGE,** born in Dublin, settled in Philadelphia as
a shipbuilder, Loyalist, settled in Halifax, Nova Scotia,
by 1786. [PRO.AO12.75.1]

**MORGAN, GEORGE,** from Ireland, settled in March, Ontario,
on 23 August 1820. [PAO.MS154]

**MORGAN, NELL,** an Irish servant who absconded from George Donald in Richmond, Virginia, in March 1766. [VaGaz.7.3.1766]

**MORGAN, THOMAS,** from Ireland, settled in March, Ontario, on 2 September 1822. [PAO.MS154]

**MORIN, JAMES,** from Ireland, settled in Huntley, Ontario, on 23 August 1820. [PAO.MS154]

**MORPHY, PHELMEY,** an indentured servant who emigrated from Belfast on the Bruerton of Liverpool, master John Fowler, to Philadelphia in 1729. [PRONI#D354/71]

**MORRIS, JAMES,** from Ireland, settled in Ramsay, Ontario, on 2 April 1821. [PAO.MS154]

**MORRIS, JOHN,** from Ireland, landed from the Mary Ann on 8 August 1817, landed in Yonge, Ontario, on 16 September 1817. [PAO.MS154]

**MORRIS, JOSEPH,** settled in Beckwith, Ontario, on 19 June 1821. [PAO.MS154]

**MORRIS, THOMAS,** from Waterford on the St George of London, to Maryland in 1677. [SPDom#19/393][MSA.LO.Patents#15/553]

**MORRIS, THOMAS,** sr., arrived on the Ploughman 15 October 1817, land grant in Drummond, Ontario, 3 February 1818. [PAO.MS154]

**MORRIS or MORRISON, WILLIAM,** 5 feet 10 inches tall, an Irish indentured servant who was imprisoned in Augusta County, Virginia, in October 1771. [VaGaz.31.10.751]

**MORRISON, ROBERT,** a yeoman from Ireland, settled in Cavan, Newcastle, Ontario, on 2 November 1818. [PAO.MS154]

**MORRISON, WILLIAM,** from Ireland, settled in Cavan, Newcastle, Ontario, on 11 October 1817. [PAO.MS154]

**MORROW, JAMES,** from Ireland, settled in Dalhousie, Ontario, on 31 July 1822. [PAO.MS154]

**MORROW, JOHN,** a cabinet-maker who settled in Philadelphia by 1793. [PRONI#T3525]

**MORROW, ROBERT,** a tailor from Ireland, settled in Cavan, Newcastle, Ontario, on 11 September 1818. [PAO.MS154]

**MORTACHE, HENRY**, and his wife, arrived on the
Constantine in 1819, settled in Drummond, Ontario, 20
March 1820. [PAO.MS154]

**MORTON, EDWARD,** a merchant from Ireland, settled in
Cavan, Newcastle, Ontario, on 15 September 1818.
[PAO.MS154]

**MORTON, WILLIAM,** from Ireland, settled in Cavan,
Newcastle, Ontario, on 3 August 1818. [PAO.MS154]

**MORTON, WILLIAM,** from Ireland, settled in Goulburn,
Ontario, on 30 November 1821. [PAO.MS154]

**MOTLEY, JAMES,** and son, from Ireland, landed from the
Aid on 14 August 1817, settled in Yonge, Ontario, on
27 September 1817. [PAO.MS154]

**MOULTON, CHARLES**, with his wife and son, arrived on the
Jane 30 August 1819, land grant in Bathurst, Ontario,
14 March 1820. [PAO.MS154]

**MOULTON, JAMES,** with his wife, two sons and five
daughters, from Ireland, landed from the Fanny on 1
August 1817, settled in Yonge, Ontario, on 6 October
1817. [PAO.MS154]

**MOULTON, JOHN,** from Ireland, settled in Lanark, Ontario,
on 1 November 1821. [PAO.MS154]

**MOULTON, JOSEPH,** from Ireland, landed from the Mary
Ann on 8 August 1817, settled in Yonge, Ontario, on 6
October 1817. [PAO.MS154]

**MOULTON, JOSEPH,**from Ireland, settled in Lanark,
Ontario, on 1 November 1821. [PAO.MS154]

**MOULTON, ROBERT,** from Ireland, settled in Lanark,
Ontario, on 21 September 1821. [PAO.MS154]

**MOULTON, THOMAS,** from Ireland, settled in Lanark,
Ontario, on 21 September 1812. [PAO.MS154]

**MUB, PETER**, from Youghal to Maryland on the Encrease of
Youghal, master Philip Popplestone, in 1679.
[Dorchester Co. Patents, WC#129]
[MSA.Patents#20/184]

**MULDOON, JAMES,** from Ireland, a former soldier of the 4th
Royal Veterans, with wife, son and daughter, settled in
Beckwithwith, Ontario, 1 December 1817.
[PAO.MS154]

**MULLARONEY, MAURICE,** formerly a private of the
Glengarry Fencibles, from Ireland, settled in
Drummond, Ontario, on 23 July 1816. [PAO.MS154]

**MULLIGAN, JOHN,** from Ireland, settled in Huntley, Ontario,
on 26 November 1822. [PAO.MS154]

**MULLIGAN, THOMAS,** from Ireland, settled in Goulburn,
Ontario, on 23 August 1820. [PAO.MS154]

**MULLIGAN, THOMAS,** from Ireland, settled in Huntley,
Ontario, on 19 September 1822. [PAO.MS154]

**MULLIN, HUGH,** from Waterford on the St George of
London, to Maryland in 1677.
[SPDom#19/393][MSA.LO.Patents#15/553]

**MULLINS, PATRICK,** from Ireland, formerly in the 27th
Regiment, with his wife and son, settled in Drummond,
Ontario, 17 December 1817. [PAO.MS154]

**MULLINS, PATRICK,** sr., with his wife and two sons from
Ireland, settled in Lanark, Ontario, on 21 September
1821. [PAO.MS154]

**MULREAN, HONOR,** from Youghal to Maryland on the
Encrease of Youghal, master Philip Popplestone, in
1679. [Dorchester Co. Patents, WC#129]
[MSA.Patents#20/184]

**MULREAU, DAVID,** from Youghal to Maryland on the
Encrease of Youghal, master Philip Popplestone, in
1679. [Dorchester Co. Patents, WC#129]
[MSA.Patents#20/184]

**MULREAU, HELENA,** from Youghal to Maryland on the
Encrease of Youghal, master Philip Popplestone, in
1679. [Dorchester Co. Patents, WC#129]
[MSA.Patents#20/184]

**MURPHY, BARTHOLEMEW,** born 1801, from Clogheen,
County Cork, emigrated from Cove on the Stakesby to
Quebec on 8 July 1823, settled in Ramsay township,
Ontario. [PAO.prp]

**MURPHY, EDWARD,** from Ireland, formerly the
quartermaster sergeant of the Royal Newfoundland
Regiment, with his wife, two sons and two daughters,
settled in Drummond, Ontario, 19 January 1819.
[PAO.MS154]

**MURPHY, HAWKINS,** from Ireland, settled in Huntley,
Ontario, on 2 July 1821. [PAO.MS154]

**MURPHY, HENRY**, from Waterford on the <u>St George of London</u>, to Maryland in 1677.
[SPDom#19/393][MSA.LO.Patents#15/553]

**MURPHY, JAMES,** born 1724, a tailor and indentured servant who absconded from George Long in Maryland in April 1754. [MsGaz#468]

**MURPHY, JAMES,** a yeoman from Ireland, settled in Cavan, Newcastle, Ontario, on 2 November 1818.
[PAO.MS154]

**MURPHY, JANE**, from Waterford on the <u>St George of London</u>, to Maryland in 1677.
[SPDom#19/393][MSA.LO.Patents#15/553]

**MURPHY, JOHN,** born in Ireland, 5 feet 4 inches tall, an indentured servant and joiner, absconded from John Patterson in Alexandria, Fairfax County, Virginia, in July 1760. [MdGaz#798]

**MURPHY, JOHN,** from Ireland, settled in Goulburn, Ontario, on 30 January 1820. [PAO.MS154]

**MURPHY, JOHN,** settled in Drummond, Ontario, on 30 March 1821. [PAO.MS154]

**MURPHY, JOHN,** landed from the <u>Britain</u> on 7 June 1821, settled in Shelbourne, Ontario, on 3 December 1821.
[PAO.MS154]

**MURPHY, MARTIN,** formerly a private of the 37TH Regiment, from Ireland, settled in Drummond, Ontario, on 16 July 1816. [PAO.MS154]

**MURPHY, MATTHEW,** from Ireland, settled in Cavan, Newcastle, Ontario, on 15 December 1817.
[PAO.MS154]

**MURPHY, MICHAEL,** formerly a private of the Glengarry Fencibles, from Ireland, settled in Drummond, Ontario, on 16 July 1816. [PAO.MS154]

**MURPHY, MORTAGH,** from Youghal to Maryland on the <u>Encrease of Youghal</u>, master Philip Popplestone, in 1679. [Dorchester Co. Patents, WC#129]
[MSA.Patents#20/184]

**MURPHY, PATRICK,** from Ireland, settled in Dalhousie, Ontario, on 24 September 1821. [PAO.MS154]

**MURPHY, THOMAS**, late of the Royal Sappers, with his wife, a son and two daughters, settled in Lanark, Ontario, 1 November 1820. [PAO.MS154]

**MURPHY, THOMAS,** from Ireland, settled in Huntley, Ontario, on 2 July 1821. [PAO.MS154]

**MURPHY, WILLIAM,** from Ireland, settled in Cavan, Newcastle, Ontario, on 15 September 1818. [PAO.MS154]

**MURRAY, Dr HUGH,** born in Ireland during 1741, died in Bethlem, Connecticut, on 28 August 1815. [GM.85.634]

**MURRAY, MICHAEL,** born in Ireland during 1746, 5 feet 9 inches tall, an indentured servant who absconded from Edward Stevenson, Frederick County, Virginia, in June 1767. [VaGaz.11.6.1767]

**MURRAY, WILLIAM,** formerly a private of the 88th Regiment, from Ireland, settled in Beckwith, Ontario, on 28 February 1817. [PAO.MS154]

**MURREL, CATHERINE,** an indentured servant who emigrated from Ireland on the Providence of Dublin, 160 tons, master John Hamilton, and arrived in the Rappahannock River, Virginia, on 30 March 1699. [XJVa.I.458]

**MURROE, JOHN,** an Irish indentured servant who absconded from Matthew Kenner, Wiccocomoco River, Virginia, on 22 October 1738. [VaGaz.3.11.1738]

**NAGLE, GARRET,** with Honorah, Garret jr., Richard, John, Patrick, Michael, James and Maryanne, from Fermoy, County Cork, emigrated from the Cove of Cork on the Hebe bound for Quebec on 8 July 1823, settled in Ramsay township, Ontario. [PAO.prp]

**NAGLE, MICHAEL,** born 1788, with his wife Mary born 1791, and children David born 1813, Ellen born 1815, Mary born 1817, and Morris born 1820, from Mallow, County Cork, emigrated from Cove on the Stakesby to Quebec on 8 July 1823, settled in Bathurst, Ontario. [PAO.prp]

**NAIL, HONOR,** an indentured servant who emigrated from Limerick to America on the Industry of Westhaven, master James Lowes, in March 1774. [Hook pp, DU]

**NAILES, JOHN,** born 1734, an indentured servant who absconded from Neal Clark and John Welsh in Anne Arundel County, Maryland, on 30 March 1752. [MdGaz#365]

**NANURY, THOMAS**, from Youghal to Maryland on the Encrease of Youghal, master Philip Popplestone, in 1679. [Dorchester Co. Patents, WC#129] [MSA.Patents#20/184]

**NEAL, JOHN,** born around 1719, an Irish indentured servant, absconded from Stephen Onion, Gunpowder Iron Works, Maryland, on 24 March 1747. [MdGaz#102]

**NEALE, HONORA**, from Youghal to Maryland on the Encrease of Youghal, master Philip Popplestone, in 1679. [Dorchester Co. Patents, WC#129] [MSA.Patents#20/184]

**NEALE, WILLIAM,** an Irish indentured servant who absconded from William Ficklin in King George County, Virginia, in 1746. [VaGaz.11.9.1746]

**NEIL, JAMES**, from Ireland, settled in Monaghan, Newcastle, Ontario, on 11 November 1817. [PAO.MS154]

**NEIL, ......,** with his children, emigrated from Belfast on 27 September 1795 aboard the America bound fro Boston, arrived there on 12 December 1795. [PRONI#D394/2]

**NEILSON, JAMES,** an indentured servant who emigrated from Belfast on the Bruerton of Liverpool, master John Fowler, to Philadelphia in 1729. [PRONI#D354/71]

**NELLIGAN, PATRICK,** born 1800, from Doneraile, County Cork, emigrated from Cove on the Stakesby to Quebec on 8 July 1823, settled in Huntley, Ontario. [PAO.prp]

**NELSON, JAMES,** from County Antrim, a mariner on HMS Garland, probate 25 April 1767 New York.

**NELSON, PETER,** born in Ireland during 1851, a labourer who emigrated via Glasgow, Scotland, to Halifax, Nova Scotia, on the SS Manitoban in April 1881. [PANS]

**NESBIT, ROBERT,** a yeoman from Ireland, settled in Toronto, Home, Ontario, on 22 April 1819. [PAO.MS154]

**NESBITT, GEORGE,** landed from the Convely on 24 July 1821, settled in Beckwith, Ontario, on 4 December 1821. [PAO.MS154]

**NESBITT, JOHN,** landed from the Convely on 24 July 1821, settled in Beckwith, Ontario, on 4 December 1821. [PAO.MS154]

**NESBITT, WILLIAM,** and his wife, landed from the Convely on 24 July 1821, settled in Beckwith, Ontario, on 4 December 1821. [PAO.MS154]

**NEWLAND, ANDREW,** from Ireland, settled in Toronto, Home, Ontario, on 22 April 1819. [PAO.MS154]

**NEWMARCH, WILLIAM,** from Youghal to Maryland on the Encrease of Youghal, master Philip Popplestone, in 1679. [Dorchester Co. Patents, WC#129] [MSA.Patents#20/184]

**NICHOLS, NATHANIEL,** an indentured servant who absconded from George Presbury, Joppa, Maryland, on 11 March 1754. [MdGaz#462]

**NICHOLSON, JOHN,** jr., from Ireland, settled in Goulburn, Ontario, on 20 February 1820. [PAO.MS154]

**NOCCOLL, MARY,** an indentured servant who emigrated from Limerick to America on the Industry of Westhaven, master James Lowes, in March 1774. [Hook pp, DU]

**NOLAN, PATRICK,** formerly a Lieutenant of the Canadian Fencibles, from Ireland, settled in Drummond, Ontario, on 16 November 1816. [PAO.MS154]

**NOLAN, PHILIP,** from Ireland, settled in Brock, Home, Ontario, on 12 August 1817. [PAO.MS154]

**NOLAND, THOMAS,** born 1746, 5 feet 10 inches tall, an Irish indentured servant and joiner who absconded from Richard Arell in Alexandria, Virginia, on 2 April 1751. [VaGaz.6.5.1771]

**NOUGHTAN, THOMAS,** 5 feet 8 inches tall, an Irish indentured servant who absconded from John Thompson in prince Edward County, Virginia, in November 1774. [VaGaz.17.11.1774]

**NOWLAN, JOHN,** from Ireland, settled in Beckwith, Ontario, on 23 August 1820. [PAO.MS154]

**NOWLAND, SHILLAM,** from Waterford on the St George of London, to Maryland in 1677. [SPDom#19/393][MSA.LO.Patents#15/553]

**NOWLAND, THOMAS**, from Waterford on the <u>St George of London</u>, to Maryland in 1677.
[SPDom#19/393][MSA.LO.Patents#15/553]

**NUGENT, ARTHUR,** and his wife, from Ireland, settled in Ramsay, Ontario, on 30 November 1821.
[PAO.MS154]

**NUGENT, THOMAS,** from Streamstown, County Meath, then a merchant in London, later a planter in Montserrat, 1698. [ActsPCCol.1698#698]

**NUNAN, JOHN,** born 1801, with his wife Katherine born 1801, and daughter Mary born 1821, from Mallow in County Cork, emigrated from Cove on the <u>Stakesby</u> to Quebec on 8 July 1823, settled in Huntley, Ontario.
[PAO.prp]

**NURANE, DENNIS,** from Youghal to Maryland on the <u>Encrease of Youghal</u>, master Philip Popplestone, in 1679. [Dorchester Co. Patents, WC#129]
[MSA.Patents#20/184]

**NUTER, LENNARD,** from Ireland, settled in Cavan, Newcastle, Ontario, on 16 October 1817. [PAO.MS154]

**O'BRIEN, J. H.,** formerl an Ensign of the Royal Newfoundland Fencibles, from Ireland, settled in Drummond, Ontario, on 26 June 1817. [PAO.MS154]

**O'BRIEN, JOHN,** born 1789, from Kanturk, County Cork, emigrated from Cove on the <u>Stakesby</u> to Quebec on 8 July 1823, settled in Ramsay township, Ontario.
[PAO.prp]

**O'BRIEN, JOSEPH,** formerly an Ensign,with his wife and daughter, from Ireland, settled in Elmsley and Beckwithwith, Ontario, on 30 November 1816.
[PAO.MS154]

**O'BRIEN, THOMAS,** from Mallow, County Cork, emigrated from Cove on the <u>Stakesby</u> to Quebec on 8 July 1823, settled in Ramsay township, Ontario. [PAO.prp]

**O'BRIEN, TIMOTHY,** born 1791, with his wife Katherine born 1795, and children Pat born 1814, Joanna born 1815, Jeremiah born 1818, and Julia born 1821, from Liscarrol, County Cork, emigrated from Cove on the <u>Stakesby</u> to Quebec on 8 July 1823, settled in Ramsay township, Ontario. [PAO.prp]

**O'BRYAN, JAMES**, born 1728, a convict indentured servant, absconded from John Ashford, Cecil County, Maryland, on 7 May 1750. [MdGaz#285]

**O'BRYAN, LAWRENCE,** born 1731, an Irish indentured servant who had arrived in the Patapsco River that summer, absconded from John Dorsey and John Carr near Elk Ridge, Ann Arundel County, Maryland, in August 1757. [Md Gaz#644]

**O'BRYEN, MORGAN**, a planter in St Kitts, 1661. [ActsPCCol.1661#520]

**O'CAHILL, JAMES**, from Waterford on the St George of London, to Maryland in 1677. [SPDom#19/393][MSA.LO.Patents#15/553]

**O'CALLAGHAN, PATRICK,** an Irish indentured servant in Barbados, 1657. [Minutes of the Council of Barbados, 16.12.1657]

**O'CONNOR, FRANCIS,** an Irish indentured servant who absconded from Thomas Nevitt in Cambridge, Virginia, on 12 October 1736. [VaGaz.15.10.1736]

**O'CONNOR, JOHN,** from Ireland, settled in Lanark, Ontario, on 3 November 1821. [PAO.MS154]

**O'CONNOR, LEWIS,** from Ireland, settled in Goulburn, Ontario, on 30 November 1821. [PAO.MS154]

**O'CONNOR, RICHARD,** from Ireland, a former clerk of the Commissary Department, settled in Drummond, Ontario, 25 May 1818. [PAO.MS154]

**O'DONAUGH, JAMES,** a weaver from Ireland, settled in Smith, Newcastle, Ontario, on 5 January 1819. [PAO.MS154]

**O'DONELL, PETER,** a yeoman from Ireland, settled in Smith, Newcastle, Ontario, on 5 January 1819. [PAO.MS154]

**O'FEE, TIMOTHY,** from Ireland, settled in Cavan, Newcastle, Ontario, on 15 December 1817. [PAO.MS154]

**OGAN, WILLIAM**, from Waterford on the St George of London, to Maryland in 1677. [SPDom#19/393][MSA.LO.Patents#15/553]

**OGLE, THOMAS,** 5 feet 6 inches tall, a shoemaker and indentured servant from Ireland who absconded from Benjamin Johnston in Fredericksburg, Virginia, during 1774. [VaGaz.20.10.1774]

**O'HARA, THOMAS,** formerly a sergeant of the Glengarry
Fencibles, with his wife, from Ireland, settled in
Burgess, Ontario, on 22 August 1816. [PAO.MS154]

**O'HARE, JAMES,** a surgeon, arrived on the Ploughman 15
October 1817, land grant in Oxford, Ontario, 1
December 1818. [PAO.MS154]

**O'HEARA, THOMAS,** a former sergeant of the Glengarry
Fencibles, from Ireland, settled in Leeds, Ontario, on
31 July 1817. [PAO.MS154]

**OLIVER, ROBERT,** a linen weaver, from Dublin to North
Carolina on the George of Dublin, master Thomas
Cumming, in 1735. [ICJ]

**O'MEHAGEN, DANIEL,** a free person from Ireland, arrived
in Barbados during 1654. [Minutes of the Council of
Barbados, 6.12.1654]

**O'NEALE, HARRY,** born around 1729, a weaver and
indentured servant, absconded from John Connor,
Kent County, Chester Town, Maryland, in April 1748.
[MdGaz#155]

**O'NEIL, CORNELIUS,** born 1720, 5 feet 7 inches tall, an
Irish indentured servant who absconded from James
Mills, St Mary's County, Maryland, on 22 April 1760.
[MdGaz#782]

**O'NEIL, NEIL,** with his wife and two daughters from Ireland,
settled in Dalhousie, Ontario, on 3 December 1821.
[PAO.MS154]

**O'NEIL, PATRICK,** from Ireland, settled in Dalhousie,
Ontario, on 27 July 1822. [PAO.MS154]

**O'NEILL, JAMES,** from Ireland, settled in Marlborough,
Ontario, on 2 November 1822. [PAO.MS154]

**ORMSBY, EDWARD,** an Irish indentured servant and tailor
who absconded from William Johnston in
Westmoreland County, Virginia, on 21 December 1738.
[VaGaz.27.1.1738]

**ORR, WILLIAM,** from Ireland, settled in Cavan, Ontario, on 9
September 1817. [PAO.MS154]

**OSBORN, RICHARD,** from Ireland, settled in Ramsay,
Ontatio, on 6 May 1821. [PAO.MS154]

**OSBORNE, WILLIAM,** emigrated via Portrush on 27 August
1768 on the Providence, master Thomas Clark, bound

for New York, shipwrecked on 8 September.
[BNL#3283, 3.2.1769]

**OSBURNE, GEORGE,** from Ireland, settled in Cavan,
Newcastle, Ontario, on 12 September 1817.
[PAO.MS154]

**O'SULLIVAN, FLORENCE,** Captain of an Independent
Company in Barbados and Montserrat in 1666.
[ActsPCCol.1668#741/788]

**OWEN, JAMES,** from Waterford on the St George of
London, to Maryland in 1677.
[SPDom#19/393][MSA.LO.Patents#15/553]

**OXEN, WILLIAM,** 5 feet 6 inches, an Irish runaway servant
who was imprisoned in Williamsburg jail, Virginia
during August 1746. [VaGaz.21.8.1746]

**PALMER, WILLIAM,** a former private of the 104th Regiment,
with his wife, two sons and three daughters, from
Ireland, settled in Burgess, Ontario, on 30 June 1817.
[PAO.MS154]

**PARK, ROBERT,** a mason from Ireland, settled in Smith,
Newcastle, Ontario, on 20 October 1818. [PAO.MS154]

**PARKS, JOHN,** a yeoman from Ireland, settled in Cavan,
Newcastle, Ontario, on 22 August 1818. [PAO.MS154]

**PASSMORE, NICHOLAS,** from Ireland, settled in Cavan,
Newcastle, Ontario, on 15 June 1818. [PAO.MS154]

**PATERSON, DAVID,** a former army private, from Ireland,
settled in Beckwith, Ontario, on 7 March 1817.
[PAO.MS154]

**PATRICK, MATTHEW,** a former sergeant of the 3rd
Dragoons, and his wife, land grant in Beckwith,
Ontario, 18 September 1819. [PAO.MS154]

**PATTERSON, RICHARD,** from Ireland, a former private of
the 23rd Regiment, with his wife and three sons. settled
in Bathurst, Ontario, on 31 July 1817. [PAO.MS154]

**PEARSON, HENRY,** from Ireland, settled in Toronto, Home,
Ontario, on 22 April 1819. [PAO.MS154]

**PERRY, JOHN,** gentleman, Knocklofty, County Tipperary,
purchased land in West New Jersey, 1664.
[NYGBR#30]

**PHELAN, JOHN,** born 1786, with his wife Katherine born
1788, and children Denis born 1809, Michael born
1814, Ellen born 1816, Joanna born 1818, John born

1819, and Pat born 1821, from Kilmore, County
Tipperaray, emigrated from Cove on the <u>Stakesby</u> to
Quebec on 8 July 1823, settled in Ramsay township,
Ontario. [PAO.prp]

**PHILLIPS, JAMES,** born around 1717, an Irish indentured
servant, absconded from William McClean, Chester
town, Maryland, on 7 June 1747. [MdGaz#112]

**PHILLIPS, .........,** from Ireland, formerly in the Royal Navy,
settled in Drummond, Ontario, 21 December 1818.
[PAO.MS154]

**PIERCE, JOHN,** from Ireland, settled in Goulburn, Ontario,
on 1 September 1822. [PAO.MS154]

**PIKE, JOHN,** gentleman, Widdingstone, County Tipperary,
purchased land in West New Jersey in 1664.
[NYGBR#30]

**PLUNKETT, GARRETT,** a free person, arrived in Barbados
from Ireland in 1654. [Minutes of the Barbados Council,
6.12.1654]

**POLLOCK, DAVID,** possibly from Templemoyle,
Limnavady, County Londonderry, settled in
Chambersburg, Pennsylvania, by 1787.
[PRONI#T1227/1]

**POLLOCK, JOHN,** from Ireland, settled in Marlborough,
Ontario, on 30 October 1822. [PAO.MS154]

**POOL, JOHN,** from Ireland, settled in Beckwith, Ontario, on
30 August 1821. [PAO.MS154]

**POOLE, GEORGE,** arrived on the <u>Atlantic</u> on 23 June 1819,
land grant in Drummond, Ontario, 8 March 1820.
[PAO.MS154]

**POOLE, JACOB,** arrived on the <u>Atlantic</u> 23 June 1819, land
grant in Drummond, Ontario, 8 March 1820.
[PAO.MS154]

**POOLE, THOMAS,** arrived on the <u>Atlantic</u> on 23 June 1819,
land grant in Drummond, Ontario, 8 March 1820.
[PAO.MS154]

**POOLE, WILLIAM,** with his wife and four sons, from Ireland,
landed from the <u>Mary Bell</u> on 8 July 1817, settled in
Yonge Escott, Ontario, on 7 October 1817.
[PAO.MS154]

**PORTER, LIZZIE,** daughter of William Porter, from Kilree,
Jerrit's Pass, Ireland, married James Smith jr. from

Edinburgh then in Cincinatti, in Indianapolis, Indiana, on 7 August 1882. [S#12,205]

**PORTER, WILLIAM,** settled in Enon Valley, Lawrence County, Pennsylvania, son of William Porter {1760-1827} and Mary Perry {1765-1838}. [Killinchy g/s, County Down]

**POWELL, JAMES H.,** from Ireland, a former Major of the 103<sup>rd</sup> Regiment, with his wife, four daughters and four sons, settled in Bathurst, Ontario, 26 August 1818, and in Drummond, Ontario, 22 June 1822. [PAO.MS154]

**POWELL, JOHN,** from Waterford on the St George of London, to Maryland in 1677. [SPDom#19/393][MSA.LO.Patents#15/553]

**POWER, DANIEL,** from Ireland, settled in Cavan, Newcastle, Ontario, on 21 May 1818. [PAO.MS154]

**POWER, JOHN,** from Waterford on the St George of London, to Maryland in 1677. [SPDom#19/393][MSA.LO.Patents#15/553]

**POWER, LAWRENCE,** from Ireland, settled in Cavan, Newcastle, Ontario, on 4 October 1817. [PAO.MS154]

**POWER, MAURICE,** formerly an army private, from Ireland, settled in Drummond, Ontario, on 14 October 1816. [PAO.MS154]

**POWER, RICHARD,** with his wife, from Ireland, settled in Ramsay, Ontario, on 12 November 1821. [PAO.MS154]

**POWER, THOMAS,** a merchant from the Isle of Speike, County Cork, was captured by a Dutch privateer when returning from the West Indies and taken to Amsterdam in 1666, his wife Ellen petitioned the King in July 1666. [SPDom#1666/577]

**POWLSON, SIMON,** born 1738, Mary born 1737, and Rose born 1765, arrived in South Carolina in January 1768 on the brigantine Chichester, master William Reid, from Belfast. [SCCJ.34.1]

**PRENDERGAST, CHARLES,** formerly a private of the Glengarry Fencibles, from Ireland, settled in Drummond, Ontario, on 17 July 1816. [PAO.MS154]

**PRENDERGAST, JAMES,** born 1786, from County Monaghan, an army lieutenant who settled in Canada, died 1834. [PRONI#D729]

**PRENDERGAST, ROBERT,** from Waterford on the St George of London, to Maryland in 1677. [SPDom#19/393][MSA.LO.Patents#15/553]

**PRESTON, ANN,** from Waterford on the St George of London, to Maryland in 1677. [SPDom#19/393][MSA.LO.Patents#15/553]

**PRINCE, MARGARET,** from Waterford on the St George of London, to Maryland in 1677. [SPDom#19/393][MSA.LO.Patents#15/553]

**PRINGLE, WILLIAM,** formerly a private of the Glengarry Fencibles, from Ireland, settled in Drummond, Ontario, on 18 July 1816. [PAO.MS154]

**PROCTER, ROBERT,** born 1711, Mary born 711, James born 1741, Rose born 1748, Mary born 1751, and Margaret born 1754, arrived in South Carolina in January 1768 on the brigantine Chichester, master William Reid, from Belfast. [SCCJ.34.1]

**PROCTER, SAMUEL,** born 1713, Catherine born 1723, Sarah born 1749, Samuel born 1751, Catherine born 1753, Philip born 1755, Edward born 1757, and Mary born 1766, arrived in South Carolina in January 1768 on the brigantine Chichester, master William Reid, from Belfast. [SCCJ.34.1]

**PROCTER, WILLIAM,** born 1717, Elizabeth born 1717, William born 1750, John born 1754, and Samuel born 1755, arrived in South Carolina in January 1768 on the brigantine Chichester, master William Reid, from Belfast. [SCCJ.34.1]

**PULLY, JOAN,** from Youghal to Maryland on the Encrease of Youghal, master Philip Popplestone, in 1679. [Dorchester Co. Patents, WC#129][MSA.Patents#20/184]

**PURFIELD, JOHN,** arrived in Maryland in 1745 from Dublin, a tailor and indentured servant who absconded from Mathew Hopkins, Rock Creek, Prince George County, Maryland, 19 September 1748. [MdGaz#179]

**QUAIL, JAMES,** from Ireland, a former sergeant of the Royal Artillery, with his wife, settled in Drummond, Ontario, on 22 August 1817, and in Leeds, Ontario, 30 November 1817. [PAO.MS154]

**QUAINE**, ALICE, from Youghal to Maryland on the <u>Encrease of Youghal</u>, master Philip Popplestone, in 1679. [Dorchester Co. Patents, WC#129][MSA.Patents#20/184]

**QUIGLEY, AUGUSTUS**, from Waterford on the <u>St George of London</u>, to Maryland in 1677. [SPDom#19/393][MSA.LO.Patents#15/553]

**QUIGLEY, CANICE,** from Waterford on the <u>St George of London</u>, to Maryland in 1677. [SPDom#19/393][MSA.LO.Patents#15/553]

**QUIGLEY, CATE,** from Waterford on the <u>St George of London</u>, to Maryland in 1677. [SPDom#19/393][MSA.LO.Patents#15/553]

**QUIGLEY, CHARLES**, from Waterford on the <u>St George of London</u>, to Maryland in 1677. [SPDom#19/393][MSA.LO.Patents#15/553]

**QUIGLEY, DANIEL**, from Waterford on the <u>St George of London</u>, to Maryland in 1677. [SPDom#19/393][MSA.LO.Patents#15/553]

**QUIGLEY, JAMES,** from Ireland, a former sergeant of the Glengarry Fencibles, settled in Oxford, Ontario, on 31 July 1817. [PAO.MS154]

**QUIGLEY, JANE**, from Waterford on the <u>St George of London</u>, to Maryland in 1677. [SPDom#19/393][MSA.LO.Patents#15/553]

**QUIGLEY, LAURENCE**, from Waterford on the <u>St George of London</u>, to Maryland in 1677. [SPDom#19/393][MSA.LO.Patents#15/553]

**QUIGLEY, MARGARET**, from Waterford on the <u>St George of London</u>, to Maryland in 1677. [SPDom#19/393][MSA.LO.Patents#15/553]

**QUIGLEY, MATTHEW**, from Waterford on the <u>St George of London</u>, to Maryland in 1677. [SPDom#19/393][MSA.LO.Patents#15/553]

**QUIGLEY, TERENCE**, from Waterford on the <u>St George of London</u>, to Maryland in 1677. [SPDom#19/393][MSA.LO.Patents#15/553]

**QUIGLEY, THOMAS**, from Waterford on the <u>St George of London</u>, to Maryland in 1677. [SPDom#19/393][MSA.LO.Patents#15/553]

**QUIN, JOHN,** from Ireland, settled in Cavan, Ontario, on 13 October 1817. [PAO.MS154]

**QUIN, JOHN,** from Ireland, settled in Lanark, Ontario, on 20 March 1821. [PAO.MS154]

**QUIN, JOHN,** from Ireland, settled in Lanark, Ontario, on 15 October 1821. [PAO.MS154]

**QUIN, PATRICK,** from Ireland, settled in Lanark, Ontario, on 15 October 1821. [PAO.MS154]

**QUIN, TIMOTHY,** born 1783, with wife Mary born 1795, and children Katherine born 1818, John born 1820, and Pat born 1822, from Rathcormac, County Cork, emigrated from Cork on the Stakesby to Quebec on 8 July 1823, settled in Ramsay township, Ontario. [PAO.prp]

**RAE, ANDREW,** with his wife and son, from Ireland, settled in Ramsay, Ontario, on 2 April 1821. [PAO.MS154]

**RAHILLY, TIMOTHY,** with Mary, Jeremiah and Patrick, from Newmarket, County Cork, emigrated from the Cove of Cork on the Hebe bound for Quebec on 8 July 1823, settled in Ramsay township, Ontario. [PAO.prp]

**RALPH, ROBERT,** from Ireland, settled in March, Ontario, on 19 September 1822. [PAO.MS154]

**RATTWELL, THOMAS,** from Ireland, settled in Lanark, Ontario, on 1 November 1821. [PAO.MS154]

**RAY, JAMES,** with Mary and Margaret, from Doneraile, County Cork, emigrated from the Cove of Cork on the Hebe bound for Quebec on 8 July 1823, settled in Ramsay township, Ontario. [PAO.prp]

**REA, WILLIAM,** from Ireland, settled in Goulburn, Ontario, on 2 September 1822. [PAO.MS154]

**READY, RICHARD,** from Waterford on the St George of London, to Maryland in 1677. [SPDom#19/393][MSA.LO.Patents#15/553]

**READY, WILLIAM,** an indentured servant who emigrated from Limerick to America on the Industry of Westhaven, master James Lowes, in March 1774. [Hook pp, DU]

**REARDEN, PATRICK,** from Ireland, settled in Cavan, Newcastle, Ontario, on 20 July 1818. [PAO.MS154]

**REDMONDS, JOSEPH,** from Ireland, settled in Cavan, Newcastle, Ontario, on 3 March 1818. [PAO.MS154]

**REDMONDS, SAMUEL,** from Ireland, settled in Cavan, Newcastle, Ontario, on 3 March 1818. [PAO.MS154]

**REED, EBENEZER,** from Waterford on the St George of London, to Maryland in 1677. [SPDom#19/393] [MSA.LO.Patents#15/553]

**REED, JOHN HUME,** with his son and daughter, arrived on the Ploughman on 15 October 1817, land grant in Drummond, Ontario, 11 February 1818. [PAO.MS154]

**REGAN, JOHN,** a former private of the Glengarry Regiment, from Ireland, settled in Drummond, Ontario, on 16 July 1816. [PAO.MS154]

**REGAN, MICHAEL,** born 1795, from Mallow, County Cork, emigrated from Cove on the Stakesby to Quebec on 8 July 1823, settled in Ramsay township, Ontario. [PAO.prp]

**REID, JAMES,** a yeoman from Ireland, settled in Smith, Newcastle, Ontario, on 19 January 1819. [PAO.MS154]

**REID, PETER,** from Ireland, settled in Cavan, Newcastle, Ontario, on 20 September 1817. [PAO.MS154]

**REILLY, CONNOR,** with his wife and son, from Ireland, settled in Dalhousie, Ontario, on 10 May 1821. [PAO.MS154]

**REILLY, EDWARD,** from Ireland, formerly a sergeant of the 5th Royal Veterans, settled in Bathurst, Ontario, 13 January 1818. [PAO.MS154]

**REILLY, EDWARD,** from Ireland, settled in Ramsay, Ontario, on 21 April 1821. [PAO.MS154]

**REILLY, JOHN,** a former private of the 68th Regiment, with his wife, land grant in Bathurst, Ontario, 7 June 1819. [PAO.MS154]

**REYNOLDS, JAMES,** from Ireland, settled in Cavan, Newcastle Ontario, on 12 September 1817. [PAO.MS154]

**REYNOLDS, JOHN,** born around 1733, a ship carpenter, absconded from Richard Patten, Maryland, July 1753. [MdGaz#427]

**RICE, JOHN,** formerly an army sergeant, with his wife and son, from Ireland, settled in Drummond, Ontario, on 15 October 1816. [PAO.MS154]

**RICE, JOHN,** from Ireland, a former sergeant of the Royal Newfoundland Fencibles, settled in Young, Ontario, on 31 July 1817. [PAO.MS154]

**RICHARDS, ROBERT,** from Carrickmacross, died in Kingston, Jamaica, during 1790. [GM.60.373]

**RICHARDSON, FERDINAND WILLIAM,** from Ireland, settled in March, Ontario, on 25 January 1820. [PAO.MS154]

**RICHARDSON, ROBERT,** with his wife and son, from Ireland, settled in Lanark, Ontario, on 5 September 1821. [PAO.MS154]

**RICHEY, JOSIAS,** from Ireland, settled in Lanark, Ontario, on 6 May 1821. [PAO.MS154]

**RICHEY, THOMAS,** from Ireland, settled in Lanark, Ontario, on 6 May 1821. [PAO.MS154]

**RICHEY, WILLIAM,** from Ireland, settled in Lanark, Ontatio, on 1 October 1821. [PAO.MS154]

**RICHIE, WELLESLEY,** a former sergeant of the 90th Regiment, from Ireland, settled in Elmsley, Ontario, on 31 July 1817. [PAO.MS154]

**RIDDIN, SUSANNAH,** an indentured servant who emigrated from Limerick to America on the Industry of Westhaven, master James Lowes, in March 1774. [Hook pp, DU]

**RIDDLE, H.,** settled in Pittsburgh, Pennsylvania, by 1857. [PRONI#D1859/17]

**RILEY. Mrs MARGARET,** born in Ireland around 1786, died in Lincoln County, North Carolina, on 5 September 1846. [Lincolnton Courier:2.9.1846]

**RIMINGTON, MICHAEL,** from Ireland, settled in Goulburn, Ontario, on 30 March 1820. [PAO.MS154]

**RIORDAN, DENNIS,** from Ireland, settled in Cavan, Newcastle, Ontario, on 3 October 1817. [PAO.MS154]

**RIORDAN, WILLIAM,** born 1803, from Mallow, County Cork, emigrated from Cove on the Stakesby to Quebec on 8 July 1823, settled in Ramsay township, Ontario. [PAO.prp]

**RIVINGTON, THOMAS,** formerly a private of the Glengarry Fencibles, from Ireland, settled in Drummond, Ontario, on 16 July 1816. [PAO.MS154]

**RIVINGTON, THOMAS,** from Ireland, settled in Huntley, Ontario, on 16 October 1820. [PAO.MS154]

**ROACH, DAVID**, from Waterford on the St George of London, to Maryland in 1677. [SPDom#19/393][MSA.LO.Patents#15/553]

**ROACH, JOHN,** emigrated from Cork to Philadelphia in 1768. [HSP:Orr, Dunlop and Glenholm ms]

**ROBERTS, ELIAS**, from Waterford on the St George of London, to Maryland in 1677. [SPDom#19/393][MSA.LO.Patents#15/553]

**ROBERTS, ROGER**, innkeeper, Dublin, purchased land in West New Jersey in 1664. [NYGBR#30]

**ROBINSON, JOHN**, settled in Chester County, Pennsylvania, during 1720s. [CCA.inv#157]

**ROBINSON, THOMAS,** with his wife and four daughters, from County Down, landed from the Alexander on 20 June 1815, settled in Bathurst, Ontario, on 19 July 1815. [PAO.MS154]

**ROBINSON, THOMAS**, late of the 8th Regiment, with his wife, son and daughter, land grant in Bathurst, Ontario, 6 August 1819. [PAO.MS154]

**ROBINSON, WILLIAM,** from Ireland, formerly of the 3rd Battalion, Sappers and Miners, with his wife, son and two daughters, settled in Drummond, Ontario, on 30 September 1817. [PAO.MS154]

**ROCHE, CORNELIUS,** with Bridget, John and Denis, from Doneraile, County Cork, emigrated from the Cove of Cork on the Hebe bound for Quebec on 8 July 1823, settled in Pakenham, Ontario. [PAO.prp]

**ROCHE, JAMES,** born 1784, from Michelstown, County Cork, emigrated from Cove on the Stakesby to Quebec on 8 July 1823, settled in Ramsay township, Ontario. [PAO.prp]

**ROCHE, NICHOLAS**, born 1723, from Ireland, died 31 October 1808, buried in Thompson Hill Cemetery, Plymouth, Massachusetts. [Plymouth g/s]

**RODDY, JAMES,** born in 1808, son of John Roddy {1759-1834}, died in New Orleans during April 1836. [Comber g/s]

**ROGERS, JOHN,** from Waterford on the St George of London, to Maryland in 1677. [SPDom#19/393][MSA.LO.Patents#15/553]

**ROGERS, JOHN,** emigrated via Portrush on 27 August 1768 on the Providence, master Thomas Clark, bound for New York, shipwrecked on 8 September. [BNL#3283, 3.2.1769]

**ROGERS, ROBERT,** wife, family, and nine men, from Cork to Barbados on the Arabella, master John Lethun, in 1689. [ActsPCCol.1689#274/10]

**RONAN, HUGH,** from Ireland, settled in Huntley, Ontario, on 16 October 1820. [PAO.MS154]

**ROONEY, WILLIAM,** a farmer in St Paul, Nebraska, by 1887, son of John Rooney a farmer in Killaney, County Down, who died 25 November 1884. [NAS.SH.10.5.1887]

**ROSS, JOHN,** from Ireland, settled in Brock, Home, Ontario, on 11 October 1817. [PAO.MS154]

**ROSS, PETER,** a blacksmith and indentured servant who absconded from Cornelius Howard, near Annapolis, Maryland, on 18 March 1751. [Md Gaz#309]

**ROURKE, PATRICK,** from Ireland, formerly a private of the 81$^{st}$ Regiment, settled in Beckwithwith, Ontario, 14 March 1818. [PAO.MS154]

**ROURKE, PATRICK,** and Ellen Rourke, from Newcastle, County Limerick, emigrated from the Cove of Cork on the Hebe bound for Quebec on 8 July 1823, settled in Ramsay township, Ontario. [PAO.prp]

**ROWAN, MATTHEW,** from County Antrim, Surveyor General of North Carolina and agent for Arthur Dobbs, 1751. [PRONI#D162/52]

**ROWSON, HENRY,** from Ireland, settled in Ramsay, Ontario, on 6 May 1821. [PAO.MS154]

**ROXBROUGH, WILLIAM,** a weaver from Ireland, settled in Smith, Newcastle, Ontario, on 5 January 1819. [PAO.MS154]

**ROYALL, WILLIAM,** an indentured servant who emigrated from Limerick to America on the Industry of Westhaven, master James Lowes, in March 1774. [Hook pp, DU]

**RUBY, JOHN,** born 1806, from Mallow, County Cork, emigrated from Cove on the Stakesby to Quebec on 8 July 1823, settled in Ramsay township, Ontario. [PAO.prp]

**RUSSELL, GARRETT**, from Waterford on the St George of London, to Maryland in 1677. [SPDom#19/393][MSA.LO.Patents#15/553]

**RUSSELL, JAMES,** in New York, son of George Russell {1795-1872} and Margaret Russell {1804-1835}. [Drumbo g/s, County Down]

**RUSSELL, KATHERINE,** born 1727 in Ireland, an indentured servant who absconded from John Smith jr in Orange County, Virginia, on 20 June 1745. [VaGaZ.24.10.1745]

**RUTLEDGE, JOHN,** a yeoman from Ireland, settled in Toronto, Home, Ontario, on 22 April 1819. [PAO.MS154]

**RYAN, DANIEL,** born 1786, with wife Mary born 1788, and children Mary born 1811, Bridget born 1815, Con. born 1817, and John born 1821, from Kanturk, County Cork, emigrated from Cove on the Stakesby to Quebec on 8 July 1823, settled in Ramsay township, Ontario. [PAO.prp]

**RYAN, MARTIN,** born 1787, with wife Margaret born 1793, and children, Michael born 1811, Mort. Born 1813, Martin born 1815, John born 1817, Katherine born 1819, and James born 1821, from Six-mile Bridge, County Clare, emigrated from Cove on the Stakesby to Quebec on 8 July 1823, settled in Ramsay township, Ontario. [PAO.prp]

**RYAN, MARY**, from Waterford on the St George of London, to Maryland in 1677. [SPDom#19/393][MSA.LO.Patents#15/553]

**RYAN, PATRICK**, from Waterford on the St George of London, to Maryland in 1677. [SPDom#19/393][MSA.LO.Patents#15/553]

**RYAN, PATRICK,** an indentured servant who emigrated from Limerick to America on the Industry of Westhaven, master James Lowes, in March 1774. [Hook pp, DU]

**RYAN, PATRICK,** from Ireland, imprisoned in Williamsburg, Virginia, during October 1774. [VaGaz.27.10.1774]

**RYAN, PHILLIP,** from Ireland, formerly the Adjutant of the 10th Regiment, settled in Montague, Oxford, Ontario, 16 March 1818. [PAO.MS154]

**RYAN, THOMAS,** 5 feet 5 inches tall, an Irish indentured servant who absconded from King William County, Virginia, during 1752. [VaGaz.18.6.1752]

**RYAN, WILLIAM,** born 1729, an Irish indentured servant and wigmaker who absconded from W. Battersby in Cumberland County, Virginia, during 1752. [VaGaz.10.11.1752]

**RYAN, WILLIAM,** from Croom, County Limerick, emigrated from the Cove of Cork on the Hebe bound for Quebec on 8 July 1823, settled in Ontario. [PAO.prp]

**RYAN, .....,** formerly a private of the 37th Regiment, with his wife and daughter, settled in Bathurst, Ontario, 11 March 1820. [PAO.MS154]

**RYE, JOHN,** from Youghal to Maryland on the Encrease of Youghal, master Philip Popplestone, in 1679. [Dorchester Co. Patents, WC#129] [MSA.Patents#20/184]

**RYLEY, DENNIS,** an indentured servant who absconded from George Neall, West River, Maryland, on 21 July 1755. [MdGaz#534]

**ST CLARE, THOMAS,** an indentured servant who emigrated from Limerick to America on the Industry of Westhaven, master James Lowes, in March 1774. [Hook pp, DU]

**SALTER, WILLIAM,** from Ireland, settled in Beckwith, Ontario, on 2 November 1822. [PAO.MS154]

**SAUNDERS, JAMES,** from Ireland, settled in Beckwith, Ontario, on 31 July 1822. [PAO.MS154]

**SAUNDERS, WILLIAM,** from Ireland, settled in Beckwith, Ontario, on 31 July 1822. [PAO.MS154]

**SAVAGE, WILLIAM,** an indentured servant who emigrated from Belfast on the Bruerton of Liverpool, master John Fowler, to Philadelphia in 1729. [PRONI#D354/71]

**SCANLAN, DARBY,** an indentured servant who emigrated from Limerick to America on the Industry of

Westhaven, master James Lowes, in March 1774.
[Hook pp, DU]

**SCANLAN, MARY,** an indentured servant who emigrated from Limerick to America on the Industry of Westhaven, master James Lowes, in March 1774.
[Hook pp, DU]

**SCANLON, WILLIAM,** and his wife, from Ireland, settled in Lanark, Ontario, on 15 October 1821. [PAO.MS154]

**SCARLET, DAVID,** a weaver from Ireland, settled in Cavan, Newcastle, Ontario, on 15 September 1818.
[PAO.MS154]

**SCHARF, BEECHAM,** from Ireland, settled in March, Ontario, on 23 August 1820. [PAO.MS154]

**SCHARF, G.,** from Ireland, settled in March, Ontario, on 12 July 1822. [PAO.MS154]

**SCOLLARD, JOHN,** from Ireland, settled in Cavan, Newcastle, Ontario, on 2 September 1818.
[PAO.MS154]

**SCOLLARD, WILLIAM,** from Ireland, settled in Cavan, Newcastle, Ontario, on 2 September 1818.
[PAO.MS154]

**SCOTT, ANDREW,** from Ireland, settled in Toronto, Home, Ontario, on 22 April 1819. [PAO.MS154]

**SCOTT, JAMES,** from Ireland, settled in Beckwith, Ontario, on 12 August 1822. [PAO.MS154]

**SCOTT, JOHN,** from Ireland, settled in Huntley, Ontario, on 16 October 1820. [PAO.MS154]

**SCOTT, SAMUEL,** born during 1777 in Tullyquilly, County Down, a merchant in Charleston, South Carolina, died on 23 September 1792, buried in the Old Scots Church there. [Charleston g/s]

**SCREWTON, ANN,** from Waterford on the St George of London, to Maryland in 1677.
[SPDom#19/393][MSA.LO.Patents#15/553]

**SCREWTON, MARY,** from Waterford on the St George of London, to Maryland in 1677.
[SPDom#19/393][MSA.LO.Patents#15/553]

**SCREWTON, THOMAS,** from Waterford on the St George of London, to Maryland in 1677.
[SPDom#19/393][MSA.LO.Patents#15/553]

**SEALY, JOHN,** from Waterford on the <u>St George of London</u>, to Maryland in 1677.
[SPDom#19/393][MSA.LO.Patents#15/553]

**SEMPLE, THOMAS,** from Ireland, settled in Brock, Ontario, on 2 May 1818. [PAO.MS154]

**SHANAHAN, DENIS,** born 1802, from Charleville, County Cork, emigrated from Cove to the <u>Stakesby</u> to Quebec on 8 July 1823, settled in Pakenham, Ontario.
[PAO.prp]

**SHANLY, COOTE NISBETT,** born in Abbey of Stradbelly, Queen's County, 2 March 1819, died in Kenosha, Wisconsin, 5 April 1874. [EC#28945][S#9597]

**SHANNAN, JAMES,** from Ireland, settled in Cavan, Ontario, on 9 September 1817. [PAO.MS154]

**SHARP, ANTHONY,** a merchant, Dublin, purchased land in West New Jersey in 1664. [NYGBR#30]

**SHARP, DAVID,** a weaver from Ireland, settled in Cavan Newcastle, Ontario, on 9 September 1818.
[PAO.MS154]

**SHARP, THOMAS,** a woolcomber, Dublin, purchased land in West New Jersey in 1664. [NYGBR#30]

**SHARPE, JOSEPH,** from Ireland, settled in Cavan, Ontario, on 9 September 1817. [PAO.MS154]

**SHARPE, JOSEPH,** from Ireland, settled in Dalhousie, Ontario, on 6 May 1821. [PAO.MS154]

**SHAW, JAMES,** and his wife, from Ireland, landed from the <u>Prince Asturias</u> on 3 June 1817, settled in Yonge, Ontario, on 29 September 1817. [PAO.MS154]

**SHAW, JAMES,** from Ireland, settled in Ramsay, Ontario, on 15 August 1821. [PAO.MS154]

**SHAW, JAMES,** from Ireland, settled in Lanark, Ontario, on 1 October 1821. [PAO.MS154]

**SHAW, Mrs MARY,** born 1777 in County Down, emigrated to USA in 1790, married Finlay Shaw, died in Guilford County, North Carolina, on 4 January 1863. [North Carolina Presbyterian: 24.1.1863]

**SHAW, ROBERT,** from Ireland, settled in Cavan, Newcastle, Ontario, on 3 October 1817. [PAO.MS154]

**SHEA, DANIEL,** from Waterford on the <u>St George of London</u>, to Maryland in 1677.
[SPDom#19/393][MSA.LO.Patents#15/553]

**SHEA, DANIEL,** an indentured servant who emigrated from Limerick to America on the Industry of Westhaven, master James Lowes, in March 1774. [Hook pp. DU]

**SHEA, JANE,** from Waterford on the St George of London, to Maryland in 1677.
[SPDom#19/393][MSA.LO.Patents#15/553]

**SHEA, MICHAEL,** from Waterford on the St George of London, to Maryland in 1677.
[SPDom#19/393][MSA.LO.Patents#15/553]

**SHEA, ROBERT,** born 1787, with wife Mary born 1795, and son Simon born 1821, from Mallow, County Cork, emigrated from Cove on the Stakesby to Quebec on 8 July 1823, settled in Lanark, Ontario. [PAO.prp]

**SHEA, THOMAS,** from Waterford on the St George of London, to Maryland in 1677.
[SPDom#19/393][MSA.LO.Patents#15/553]

**SHEAL, ADAM,** settled in Drummond, Ontario, on 19 June 1821. [PAO.MS154]

**SHEAL, JOHN,** landed from the Maria on 22 June 1821, settled in Drummond, Ontario, on 19 June 1821. [PAO.MS154]

**SHEEHAN, TIMOTHY,** with Mary sr., Mary jr., Joanna, Maurice, Honora and Cornelius, from Liscarrol, County Cork, emigrated from the Cove of Cork on the Hebe bound for Quebec on 8 July 1823, settled in Ramsay township, Ontario. [PAO.prp]

**SHEELRY, JOHN,** an indentured servant who emigrated from Limerick to America on the Industry of Westhaven, master James Lowes, in March 1774. [Hook pp, DU]

**SHEHANE, CORNELIUS,** from Youghal to Maryland on the Encrease of Youghal, master Philip Popplestone, in 1679. [Dorchester Co. Patents, WC#129] [MSA.Patents#20/184]

**SHEHAWNE, THOMAS,** from Youghal to Maryland on the Encrease of Youghal, master Philip Popplestone, in 1679. [Dorchester Co. Patents, WC#129] [MSA.Patents#20/184]

**SHEPHERD, BENJAMIN,** from Ireland, settled in Ramsay, Ontario, on 24 March 1822. [PAO.MS154]

**SHERLOCK, JOHN,** an Irish indentured servant, absconded from John Lawson, Whitemarsh Plantation, Baltimore County, Maryland, on 21 May 1746. [MdGaz#57#]

**SHIELDS, SAMUEL,** from Ireland, settled in Marlborough, Ontario, on 2 November 1822. [PAO.MS154]

**SHIGINS, ELLINOR,** from Waterford on the <u>St George of London</u>, to Maryland in 1677.
[SPDom#19/393][MSA.LO.Patents#15/553]

**SHILLINGTON, JAMES,** from Ireland, settled in Goulburn, Ontario, on 30 November 1822. [PAO.MS154]

**SHORTIS, THOMAS,** from Ireland, settled in Cavan, Newcastle, Ontario, on 9 July 1818. [PAO.MS154]

**SIMONS, ANDREW,** from Waterford on the <u>St George of London</u>, to Maryland in 1677.
[SPDom#19/393][MSA.LO.Patents#15/553]

**SIMPLE, WILLIAM,** from Waterford on the <u>St George of London</u>, to Maryland in 1677.
[SPDom#19/393][MSA.LO.Patents#15/553]

**SIMPSON, JAMES,** from Ireland, settled in Goulburnk, Ontario, on 4 September 1822. [PAO.MS154]

**SIMPSON, SAMUEL,** from Ireland, settled in Goulburn, Ontario, on 4 September 1822. [PAO.MS154]

**SIMPSON, WILLIAM,** from Ireland, settled in Goulburn, Ontario, on 4 September 1822. [PAO.MS154]

**SINGLETON, MICHAEL,** from Ireland, settled in Goulburn, Ontario, on 22 September 1820. [PAO.MS154]

**SKERRETT, GEORGE,** a merchant in St Kitts, 1724. [NLI.ms14,165]

**SKIRLEY, WILLIAM,** from Ireland, settled in Huntley, Ontario, on 12 August 1822. [PAO.MS154]

**SLATER, ALEXANDER,** an indentured servant who emigrated from Belfast on the <u>Bruerton of Liverpool,</u> master John Fowler, to Philadelphia in 1729. [PRONI#D354/71]

**SLATTERY, PATRICK,** with Helen, Katherine, Mary and Patrick jr., from Clogheen, County Cork, emigrated from the Cove of Cork on the <u>Hebe</u> bound for Quebec on 8 July 1823, settled in Pakenham, Ontario. [PAO.prp]

**SLATTERY, PHILIP**, from Waterford on the St George of London, to Maryland in 1677. [SPDom#19/393][MSA.LO.Patents#15/553]

**SLY, HENRY,** from Ireland, settled in Ramsay, Ontario, on 2 April 1821. [PAO.MS154]

**SLY, WILLIAM,** with his wife, four sons and four daughters, from Ireland, settled in Ramsay, Ontario, on 2 April 1821. [PAO.MS154]

**SMART, GEORGE,** from Ireland, settled in Cavan, Newcastle, Ontario, on 12 September 1817. [PAO.MS154]

**SMILIE, JOHN,** emigrated from Belfast on the Sally to Philadelphia in 1762. [PRONI]

**SMITH, DANIEL,** born in Ireland, settled in Philadelphia as innkeeper of the 'Bald Eagles', Loyalist in 1776. [PRO.AO12.102.82]

**SMITH, DAVID,** born 1744, arrived in South Carolina in January 1768 on the brigantine Chichester, master William Reid, from Belfast. [SCCJ.34.1]

**SMITH, EDWARD,** with his wife, son and daughter, from Ireland, settled in Lanark, Ontario, on 15 October 1821. [PAO.MS154]

**SMITH, JAMES,** and his wife, settled in Drummond, Ontario, 10 March 1820. [PAO.MS154]

**SMITH, JAMES,** and his wife, from Ireland, settled in Ramsay, Ontario, on 23 June 1821. [PAO.MS154]

**SMITH, JOSHUA,** from Ireland, settled in March, Ontario, on 30 November 1823. [PAO.MS154]

**SMITH, LAWRENCE,** born in Ireland around 1729, 5 feet 3 inches tall, fair complexion, an indentured servant who absconded from Onion's Ironworks, Baltimore, in August 1759. [MdGaz#745]

**SMITH, PATRICK,** an indentured servant who absconded from Basil Brooke in Benedict, Maryland, on 2 February 1755. [MdGaz#523]

**SMITH, ROBERT,** an indentured servant who emigrated from Belfast on the Bruerton of Liverpool, master John Fowler, to Philadelphia in 1729. [PRONI#D354/71]

**SMITH, ROBERT,** from Ireland, settled in March, Ontario, on 23 August 1820. [PAO.MS154]

**SMITH, ROBERT,** son of James Smith in Moycraig, parish of
Billy, County Antrim, settled in Philadelphia by 1837.
[PRONI#D1828/7]

**SMITH, THOMAS,** from Youghal to Maryland on the
Encrease of Youghal, master Philip Popplestone, in
1679. [Dorchester Co. Patents, WC#129]
[MSA.Patents#20/184]

**SMYTH, JAMES,** from Youghal to Maryland on the Encrease
of Youghal, master Philip Popplestone, in 1679.
[Dorchester Co. Patents, WC#129]
[MSA.Patents#20/184]

**SMYTHE, JAMES,** with his wife, son and two daughters,
from Ireland, settled in Lanark, Ontario, on 1 November
1821. [PAO.MS154]

**SMYTH, ROBERT,** son of James Smyth, emigrated from
Moycraig, parish of Billy, County Antrim, to
Philadelphia in 1837. [PRONI#D1828/18]

**SMYTH, WILLIAM,** possibly from County Antrim, settled in
Philadelphia by 1837. [PRONI#D1828/3]

**SPEARS, ALEXANDER,** absconded from the snow Edward,
master Abraham Weddett, in the Patuxent River,
Maryland, in August 1757. [MdGaz#653]

**SPENCER, DANIEL,** born 1725, 5 feet 7 inches tall, dark
complexion, an Irish indentured servant who
absconded from Mark Kenton in Fauquier County,
Virginia, on 16 September 1770. [VaGaz.11.10.1770]

**SPINKS, HENRY,** from Ireland, settled in Cavan, Newcastle,
Ontario, on 19 March 1818. [PAO.MS154]

**SPLAIN, SAMUEL,** with his wife, two sons and one
daughter, landed from the Martha Gray in May 1821,
settled in Beckwith, Ontario, on 4 December 1821.
[PAO.MS154]

**SPRATT, HUGH,** formerly a private of the Canadian
Fencibles, from Ireland, settled in Burgess, Ontario, on
30 September 1816. [PAO.MS154]

**SPRATT, HUGH,** a former quartermaster sergeant of the
Glengarry Fencibles, from Ireland, settled in Kettley,
Ontario, on 26 June 1817. [PAO.MS154]

**SPROULE, ANDREW,** a carpenter, who settled in
Philadelphia by 1793. [PRONI#T3525]

**SPROULE, JOHN,** from Ireland, settled in Marlborough, Ontario, on 10 November 1822. [PAO.MS154]

**SPROULE, SAMUEL,** from Ireland, settled in Goulburn, Ontario, on 31 January 1821. [PAO.MS154]

**SPROULE, THOMAS,** from Ireland, settled in Goulburn, Ontario, on 20 September 1820. [PAO.MS154]

**SPROULE, WILLIAM,** from Ireland, settled in Marlborough, Ontario, on 10 November 1822. [PAO.MS154]

**STACEY, BENJAMIN,** settled in Bathurst, Ontario, on 26 June 1821. [PAO.MS154]

**STAPLES, RICHARD,** a yeoman from Ireland, settled in Cavan, Newcastle, Ontario, on 15 October 1818. [PAO.MS154]

**STAPLETON, BENJAMIN,** a yeoman from Ireland, settled in Smith, Newcastle, Ontario, on 10 December 1818. [PAO.MS154]

**STAPLETON, JOHN,** a yeoman from Ireland, settled in Smith, Newcastle, Ontario, on 10 December 1818. [PAO.MS154]

**STAPLETON, WILLIAM,** a yeoman from Ireland, settled in Smith, Newcastle, Ontario, on 10 December 1818. [PAO.MS154]

**STARKEY, THOMAS,** gentleman, Abbey Lace, Queens County, Ireland, purchased land in West New Jersey in 1664. [NYGBR#30]

**STARR, JAMES,** from Ireland, settled in Huntley, Ontario, on 16 October 1820. [PAO.MS154]

**STEDMAN, JOSEPH,** from Ireland, settled in Lanark, Ontario, on 20 March 1821. [PAO.MS154]

**STEEL, JOHN,** born 1740, emigrated from Belfast on the Chichester, William Reed, to South Carolina, arrived in January 1768. [SCCJ.IV.1]

**STEELE, WILLIAM,** merchant, Cork, purchased land in West New Jersey in 1664. [NYGBR#30]

**STEIL, ROBERT,** born 1719, Margaret born 1729, Nelly born 1754, James born 1760, Henry born 1763, and Elizabeth born 1764, arrived in South Carolina in January 1768 on the brigantine Chichester, master William Reid, from Belfast. [SCCJ.34.1]

**STEPHENSON, SAMUEL,** from Ireland, settled in Brock, Home, Ontario, on 14 July 1817. [PAO.MS154]

**STERNE, CHARLES,** from Ireland, settled in Ramsay, Ontario, on 14 April 1821. [PAO.MS154]

**STEVENSON, Dr HENRY,** settled in Baltimore, Maryland, in 1752, a Loyalist in 1776. [PRO.AO12.6.278]

**STEWART, GEORGE,** born in County Antrim 1801, with his wife Ann born there 1801, and sons William born there in 1821 and Samuel born at sea in 1823, emigrated to America in 1823, naturalised in Plattsbush, Clinton County, New York, in 1828. [Clinton Court book 2/544]

**STEWART, HUGH,** born in Ireland, a merchant shipmaster in Philadelphia, Loyalist in 1776. [PRO.AO12.42.380]

**STEWART, JOHN,** probably from the parish of Billy, County Antrim, settled in Philadelphia by 1837. [PRONI#D1828/7]

**STOTT, ROBERT,** an indentured servant who emigrated from Belfast on the Bruerton of Liverpool, master John Fowler, to Philadelphia in 1729. [PRONI#D354/71]

**STRONG, PETER,** born in Ireland, 5 feet 7 inches tall, fair complexion, a convict indentured servant nd a carpenter, who absconded from Baltimore, Maryland, on 5 February 1759. [MdGaz#719]

**STUART, JOHN,** from Ireland, settled in Cavan, Newcastle, Ontario, on 12 September 1817. [PAO.MS154]

**STUART, JOHN,** with his wife, son and two daughters, from Ireland, settled in Lanark, Ontario, on 24 August 1822. [PAO.MS154]

**STYLES, JOHN,** from Ireland, settled in Huntley, Ontario, on 12 August 1822. [PAO.MS154]

**SULLIVAN, DANIEL,** born 1715, an Irish carpenter and indentured servant, absconded from Samuel Smith on 9 July 1745. [MdGaz#14]

**SULLIVAN, DANIEL,** 'lately come into the country', an Irish indentured servant who absconded from Back Creek, Cecil County, Maryland, in October 1750. [MdGaz#290]

**SULLIVAN, JOHN,** from Ireland, formerly of the Royal Navy, settled in Drummond, Ontario, on 15 September1817. [PAO.MS154]

**SULLIVAN, JOHN,** born 1792, from Watersgrasshill, County Cork, emigrated from Cove on the Stakesby to Quebec

on 8 July 1823, settled in Pakenham, Ontario.
[PAO.prp]

**SULLIVAN, JOHN,** with Mary, Bess, John, Mary and Margaret, from Doneraile, County Cork, emigrated from the Cove of Cork on the Hebe bound for Quebec on 8 July 1823, settled in Pakenham, Ontario. [PAO.prp]

**SULLIVAN, MARGARET**, from Waterford on the St George of London, to Maryland in 1677.
[SPDom#19/393][MSA.LO.Patents#15/553]

**SULLIVAN, MARY**, from Waterford on the St George of London, to Maryland in 1677.
[SPDom#19/393][MSA.LO.Patents#15/553]

**SULLIVAN, PATRICK**, born 1791, with his wife Mary born 1793, and daughter Mary born 1815, from Mallow, County Cork, emigrated from Cove on the Stakesby to Quebec on 8 July 1823, settled in Pakenham, Ontario. [PAO.prp]

**SULLIVAN, WILLIAM,** from Ireland, a former private of the 58th Regiment, settled in Drummond, Ontario, 30 November 1818. [PAO.MS154]

**SUTTON, THOMAS,** from Ireland, settled in Lanark, Ontario, on 15 October 1821. [PAO.MS154]

**SWALLOW, SAMUEL**, from Waterford on the St George of London, to Maryland in 1677.
[SPDom#19/393][MSA.LO.Patents#15/553]

**SWAYNE, JOSEPH,** a shoemaker from Ireland, settled in Cavan, Newcastle, Ontario, on 15 October 1818.
[PAO.MS154]

**SWEATMAN, JEFFREY**, from Waterford on the St George of London, to Maryland in 1677.
[SPDom#19/393][MSA.LO.Patents#15/553]

**SWEENEY, DENIS,** with Mary, Margaret, Kitty, Joanna, Robert, Patrick, Cornelius and Denis, from Buttevant, County Cork, emigrated from the Cove of Cork on the Hebe bound for Quebec on 8 July 1823, settled in Ramsay township, Ontario. [PAO.prp]

**SWEENY, EDWARD,** an indentured servant who emigrated from Limerick to America on the Industry of Westhaven, master James Lowes, in March 1774.
[Hook pp, DU]

**SWENEY, EDWARD,** born in Ireland, 5 feet 5 inches tall, a felon imprisoned in Williamsburg, Virginia, in October 1774. [VaGaz.27.10.1774]

**SYMOT, DOROTHY,** from Waterford on the St George of London, to Maryland in 1677. [SPDom#19/393][MSA.LO.Patents#15/553]

**TAILOR, JOHN,** from Ireland, settled in Goulburn, Ontario, on 30 January 1820. [PAO.MS154]

**TATLOCK, SAMUEL,** from Ireland, settled in Lanark, Ontario, on 1 November 1821. [PAO.MS154]

**TAYLOR, MATTHEW,** from Ireland, settled in Huntley, Ontario, on 26 January 1821. [PAO.MS154]

**TAYLOR, RICHARD,** from Ireland, settled in Cavan, Newcastle, Ontario, on 3 August 1818. [PAO.MS154]

**TEATE, WILLIAM,** emigrated from Portrush on 27 August 1768 on the Providence, master Thomas Clark, shipwrecked on 8 September. [BNL#3283, 3.2.1769]

**TENNANT, GEORGE,** with his wife and son, from Ireland, settled in Lanark, Ontario, on 15 October 1821. [PAO.MS154]

**TENNANT, JOHN,** from Ireland, settled in Lanark, Ontario, on 17 October 1821. [PAO.MS154]

**TENNANT, RICHARD,** from Ireland, settled in Lanark, Ontario, on 17 October 1821. [PAO.MS154]

**TENNANT, THOMAS,** from Ireland, settled in Ramsay, Ontario, on 2 April 1821. [PAO.MS154]

**TENNANT, WILLIAM,** from Ireland, settled in Lanark, Ontario, on 17 October 1821. [PAO.MS154]

**THOMAS, JAMES,** with his wife, son and two daughters, from Ireland, settled in Lanark, Ontario, on 9 September 1817. [PAO.MS154]

**THOMPSON, JAMES,** born in Ireland, served in the Royal Navy during the Seven Years war, then a Customs Officer in Ireland, moved to Philadelphia, Loyalist. [PRO.AO12.100.63]

**THOMPSON, JOHN,** formerly a private of the 8th Regiment, with his wife, son and daughter, from Ireland, settled in Burgess, Ontario, on 22 August 1816. [PAO.MS154]

**THOMSON, JOHN,** a blacksmith from Ireland, settled in Ameiasburgh, Midland, Ontario, on 9 November 1818. [PAO.MS154]

**THOMSON, JOHN,** born 1793, with his wife Margaret born 1801, and daughter Martha born 1801, from Fermoy, County Cork, emigrated from Cove on the Stakesby to Quebec on 8 July 1823, settled in Ramsay township, Ontario. [PAO.prp]

**THOMPSON, MOSES,** an indentured servant who emigrated from Belfast on the Bruerton of Liverpool, master John Fowler, to Philadelphia in 1729. [PRONI#D354/71]

**THOMPSON, W. B.,** from Ireland, late of the Royal Sappers, with his wife, two sons and a daughter, settled in Dalhousie, Ontario, on 4 September 1820. [PAO.MS154]

**TIERNEY, JAMES,** with his wife, two sons and two daughters, from Ireland, settled in Lanark, Ontario, on 20 March 1821. [PAO.MS154]

**TODD, WILLIAM, sr.,** from Ireland, settled in Toronto, Home, Ontario, on 22 April 1819. [PAO.MS154]

**TODD, WILLIAM,** jr., a farmer from Ireland, settled in Toronto, Home, Ontario, on 22 April 1819. [PAO.MS154]

**TOOL, DARBY,** an Irish indentured servant and shoemaker who absconded from William Whitehead in Edgecombe Precinct, North Carolina, on 26 December 1737. [VaGaz.31.3.1737

**TOOMEY, JAMES,** from Ireland, late at Hudson Bay, settled in Home, Ontario, on 20 October 1818. [PAO.MS154]

**TOPPING, EDWARD,** with his wife and four daughters, from County Down, landed from the Alexander on 20 June 1815, settled in Bathurst, Ontario, on 19 July 1815. [PAO.MS154]

**TORNEY, JOHN,** from Ireland, settled in Huntley, Ontario, on 12 July 1822. [PAO.MS154]

**TRACEY, JAMES,** a laborer from Ireland, settled in Smith, Newcastle, Ontario, on 1 March 1819. [PAO.MS154]

**TULLY, WILLIAM,** settled in Drummond, Ontario, on 4 December 1821. [PAO.MS154]

**TURNER, ARCHIBALD,** from Ireland, settled in Lanark, Ontario, on 17 October 1821. [PAO.MS154]

**TURNER, JAMES,** from Ireland, settled in Cavan, Newcastle, Ontario, on 10 May 1818. [PAO.MS154]

**TURNER, ROBERT**, linen-draper, Dublin, purchased land in West New Jersey in 1664. [NYGBR#30]

**TUSKAY, MATTHEW,** emigrated from the Cove of Cork on the Hebe bound for Quebec on 8 July 1823, settled in Ramsay township, Ontario. [PAO.prp]

**UDELL, JOHN**, a convict indentured servant and carpenter, absconded from John Hammond and Robert Langford, Elk Ridge, Ann Arundel County, Maryland, on 22 June 1751. [MdGaz#324]

**UPTON, JOHN,** from Ireland, settled in Goulburn, Ontario, on 8 November 1821. [PAO.MS154]

**VAIL, EDMUND,** an indentured servant who emigrated from Limerick to America on the Industry of Westhaven, master James Lowes, in March 1774. [Hook pp, DU]

**VARELY, CHRISTOPHER**, from Waterford on the St George of London, to Maryland in 1677.
[SPDom#19/393][MSA.LO.Patents#15/553]

**VARELY, CHRISTY**, from Waterford on the St George of London, to Maryland in 1677.
[SPDom#19/393][MSA.LO.Patents#15/553]

**VARELY, ELIZABETH,** from Waterford on the St George of London, to Maryland in 1677.
[SPDom#19/393][MSA.LO.Patents#15/553]

**VARELY, JAMES**, from Waterford on the St George of London, to Maryland in 1677.
[SPDom#19/393][MSA.LO.Patents#15/553]

**VARELY, JANET**, from Waterford on the St George of London, to Maryland in 1677.
[SPDom#19/393][MSA.LO.Patents#15/553]

**VARELY, JOHN**, from Waterford on the St George of London, to Maryland in 1677.
[SPDom#19/393][MSA.LO.Patents#15/553]

**VAUGHAN, WILLIAM**, merchant, Clonwell, County Tipperary, purchased land in West New Jersey in 1664. [NYGBR#30]

**VENABELL, JAMES,** an Irish indentured servant, absconded from Alexander Lawson, Whitemarsh Plantation, Baltimore County, on 21 May 1746. [MdGaz#57]

**VYANS, MARGARET,** an indentured servant who absconded from John Collar and Henry Weedon, Kent Island, Maryland, in June 1753. [MdGaz.#424]

**WADE, NATHANIEL,** born in Ireland 1805, a farmer, settled in Anderson County, Texas, by 1850. [C]

**WALKER, JOHN,** born 1667, a merchant from Belfast, indented as a servant to Richard Houghton a merchant in Liverpool, emigrated via Liverpool to Virginia or Maryland 6 October 1686. [LRO.QSP#625/2]

**WALKER, JOSEPH,** from Ireland, settled in Brock, Home, Ontario, on 12 August 1817. [PAO.MS154]

**WALKER, SAMUEL,** from Ireland, settled in Dalhousie, Ontario, on 17 October 1821. [PAO.MS154]

**WALKER, THOMAS,** from Waterford on the St George of London, to Maryland in 1677.
[SPDom#19/393][MSA.LO.Patents#15/553]

**WALKER, THOMAS,** from Ireland, settled in Lanark, Ontario, on 1 November 1821. [PAO.MS154]

**WALKER, WILLIAM,** a yeoman from Ireland, settled in Toronto, Home, Ontario, on 22 April 1819. [PAO.MS154]

**WALLACE, ALEXANDER,** a tallow chandler in New York, son of James Wallace in Belfast, probate 20 November 1772 New York

**WALLACE, JOHN,** a carpenter from Ireland, settled in Toronto, Home, Ontario, on 22 April 1819. [PAO.MS154]

**WALLACE, MICHAEL,** born 1733, an indentured servant who absconded from Christopher Lowndes, Bladensburg, on 17 February 1750. [MdGaz#252]

**WALLACE, THOMAS,** from Ireland, settled in Cavan, Newcastle, Ontario, on 12 September 1817. [PAO.MS154]

**WALPOLE, WILLIAM,** landed from the brig Unity in August 1820, settled in Drummond, Ontario, on 4 December 1821. [PAO.MS154]

**WALPOLE, WILLIAM,** from Ireland, settled in Lanark, Ontario, on 1 November 1821. [PAO.MS154]

**WALSH, RICHARD,** born 1747, 5 feet 8 inches tall, fair complexion, an Irish indentured servant, gardner and ditcher who absconded from William Fleming in

Cumberland County, Virginia, on 5 June 1770.
[VaGaz.19.7.1770]

**WALSH, WILLIAM,** late of the Royal Sappers, with his wife, settled in Lanark, Ontario, 1 November 1820. [PAO.MS154]

**WALTER, WILLIAM,** a yeoman from Ireland, settled in Smith, Newcastle, Ontario, on 22 February 1819. [PAO.MS154]

**WALTON, STEPHEN,** from Waterford on the St George of London, to Maryland in 1677. [SPDom#19/393][MSA.LO.Patents#15/553]

**WARD, DAVID,** with Ally, Mary, Nora and Bess, from Newmarket, County Cork, emigrated from the Cove of Cork on the Hebe bound for Quebec on 8 July 1823, settled in Ramsay township, Ontario. [PAO.prp]

**WARD, THOMAS,** from Ireland, settled in Beckwith, Ontario, on 30 March 1820. [PAO.MS154]

**WARREN, BENJAMIN,** with his wife and two daughters, from Ireland, landed from the Mary Ann on 8 August 1817, settled in Yonge, Ontario, on 16 September 1817. [PAO.MS154]

**WARREN, BENJAMIN,** and his son, from Ireland, settled in Ramsay, Ontario, on 30 April 1822. [PAO.MS154]

**WARWICK, JANE,** from Waterford on the St George of London, to Maryland in 1677. [SPDom#19/393][MSA.LO.Patents#15/553]

**WASER, JOHN,** from Ireland, settled in Cavan, Newcastle, Ontario, on 3 October 1818. [PAO.MS154]

**WATERS, JOHN,** a blacksmith from Ireland, settled in Cavan, Newcastle, Ontario, on 19 September 1818. [PAO.MS154]

**WATSON, JAMES,** with his wife and three daughters, from Ireland, settled in Lanark, Ontario, on 24 August 1817. [PAO.MS154]

**WATTERSON, GEORGE,** from County Londonderry, settled in Stoke County, North Carolina, around 1812, naturalised in April 1824. [NCSA.CR90/3000S]

**WATTERSON, JOHN,** from County Londonderry, settled in Stoke County, North Carolina, around 1812, naturalised in April 1824. [NCSA.CR90/3000S]

**WATTS, JAMES,** from Ramelston, County Donegal, in Jamaica, 1800-1840. [PRONI#Mf135]

**WATTS, SAMUEL,** from Ramelston, County Donegal, in Barbados, 1800-1840. [PRONI#Mf135]

**WATTWOOD, GEORGE**, deserted from the Royal American Regiment in Fredericktown, Frederick County, Maryland, in August 1756. [MdGaz#591]

**WEATHERHEAD, JOHN,** from Ireland, landed from the Ocean on 22 July 1817, settled in Landsdowne, Ontario, on 4 October 1817. [PAO.MS154]

**WEBSTER, JOHN,** with his wife, two sons and one daughter, from Ireland, settled in Ramsay, Ontario, on 10 May 1821. [PAO.MS154]

**WEBSTER, THOMAS,** with his wife, two sons and two daughters from Ireland, landed from the General Moore on 8 August 1817, settled in Oxford, Ontario, on 6 October 1817. [PAO.MS154]

**WEBSTER, THOMAS,** a yeoman from Ireland, settled in Cavan, Newcastle, Ontario, on 19 September 1818. [PAO.MS154]

**WEIRDLOCK, THOMAS,** from Waterford on the St George of London, to Maryland in 1677. [SPDom#19/393][MSA.LO.Patents#15/553]

**WELCH, WALTER,** an Irish indentured servant of Edward Hollingsheade in Barbados, 1657. [Minutes of the Council of Barbados, 1.9.1657]

**WELLWOOD, ROBERT,** with his wife, two sons and two daughters, from Ireland, settled in Lanark, Ontario, on 17 October 1821. [PAO.MS154]

**WELLWOOD, SAMUEL,** from Ireland, settled in Lanark, Ontario, on 1 November 1821. [PAO.MS154]

**WELLWOOD, WILLIAM,** from Ireland, settled in Ramsay, Ontario, on 6 May 1821. [PAO.MS154]

**WELSH, ELLIS**, from Waterford on the St George of London, to Maryland in 1677. [SPDom#19/393][MSA.LO.Patents#15/553]

**WELSH, JAMES,** 5 feet 9 inches tall, an Irish indentured servant who absconded from William Forsyth in Norfolk, Virginia, in December 1774. [VaGaz.5.1.1775]

**WELSH, JANE**, from Waterford on the St George of London, to Maryland in 1677.
[SPDom#19/393][MSA.LO.Patents#15/553]

**WELSH, JOHN,** an indentured servant who emigrated from Belfast on the Bruerton of Liverpool, master John Fowler, to Philadelphia in 1729. [PRONI#D354/71]

**WELSH, JOHN**, an indentured servant who absconded from Thomas Selman, Elk Ridge, Maryland, on 22 April 1753. [MdGaz#418]

**WELSH, PHILLIP,** from Waterford on the St George of London, to Maryland in 1677.
[SPDom#19/393][MSA.LO.Patents#15/553]

**WELSH, THOMAS**, from Waterford on the St George of London, to Maryland in 1677.
[SPDom#19/393][MSA.LO.Patents#15/553]

**WELSH, WILLIAM**, from Waterford on the St George of London, to Maryland in 1677.
[SPDom#19/393][MSA.LO.Patents#15/553]

**WEST, MARGARET**, from Youghal to Maryland on the Encrease of Youghal, master Philip Popplestone, in 1679. [Dorchester Co. Patents, WC#129][MSA.Patents#20/184]

**WHEALEN, DANIEL**, born 1715, 5 feet 9 inches, an Irish convict, a smith, indentured servant, absconded from Hanover Court House in December 1745.
[MdGaz#36][VaGaz.5.12.1745]

**WHEELAN, PATRICK**, from Waterford on the St George of London, to Maryland in 1677.
[SPDom#19/393][MSA.LO.Patents#15/553]

**WHITAKER, ROBERT**, an Irish indentured servant and printer, who absconded from Peter Timothy publisher of the South Carolina Gazette in September 1751. [SCGaz]

**WHITE, JAMES,** a yeoman from Ireland, settled in Smith, Newcastle, Ontario, on 5 January 1819. [PAO.MS154]

**WHITE, JOHN,** a former sergeant of the 70th Regiment, land grant in Bathurst, Ontario, on 2 September 1819. [PAO.MS154]

**WHITE, JOHN CAMPBELL,** graduated MD from Glasgow University in 1782, possibly settled in Baltimore around 1800. [RGG.641]

**WHITE, THOMAS**, from Youghal to Maryland on the
Encrease of Youghal, master Philip Popplestone, in
1679. [Dorchester Co. Patents, WC#129]
[MSA.Patents#20/184]

**WHITMORE, WILLIAM,** with his wife, two sons and three
daughters, from Ireland, landed from the Mary Bell on 8
August 1817, settled in Yonge, Ontario, on 6 October
1817. [PAO.MS154]

**WHITNEY, RICHARD,** jr., landed from the Maria on 29 June
1819, settled in Bathurst, Ontario, on 22 February
1821. [PAO.MS154]

**WHITNEY, THOMAS,** landed from the Maria on 29 June
1819, settled in Bathurst, Ontario, on 22 February
1821. [PAO.MS154]

**WIDDESS, ROBERT,** from Ireland, settled in Cavan,
Newcastle, Ontario, on 3 August 1818. [PAO.MS154]

**WIDDESS, WILLIAM,** from Ireland, settled in Cavan,
Newcastle, Ontario, on 21 September 1817.
[PAO.MS154]

**WILEY, Mrs ANN,** born in County Antrim during 1812, died
in Charleston, South Carolina, on 27 January 1830,
buried in the Old Scots Church there. [Charleston g/s]

**WILKIN, GEORGE,** from Ireland, settled in Brock, Home,
Ontario, on 27 August 1817. [PAO.MS154]

**WILLIAMS, HERBERT,** an indentured servant who
emigrated from Limerick to America on the Industry of
Westhaven, master James Lowes, in March 1774.
[Hook pp, DU]

**WILLIAMS, JAMES,** an indentured servant who emigrated
from Limerick to America on the Industry of
Westhaven, master James Lowes, in March 1774.
[Hook pp, DU]

**WILLIAMS, JUDITH,** an indentured servant who emigrated
from Limerick to America on the Industry of
Westhaven, master James Lowes, in March 1774.
[Hook pp, DU]

**WILLIAMSON, RICHARD,** from Ireland, settled in Huntley,
Ontario, on 10 November 1821. [PAO.MS154]

**WILLIS, CATEY,** from Ireland, settled in Ramsay, Ontario,
on 10 April 1821. [PAO.MS154]

**WILLIS, JOHN**, a former sergeant of the 59th Regiment, with his wife, son and daughter, from Ireland, settled in Bathurst, Ontario, on 9 August 1817, later in Drummond, Ontario, 20 May 1820. [PAO.MS154]

**WILLIS, WILLIAM**, from Ireland, settled in Beckwith, Ontario, on 20 August 1820. [PAO.MS154]

**WILLOUGHBY, JOHN**, from Ireland, settled in Goulburn, Ontario, on 1 May 1822. [PAO.MS154]

**WILLOUGHBY, JOHN**, with his wife and son, from Ireland, landed from the Atlantic on 14 August 1817, settled in Landsdowne, Ontario, on 13 October 1817. [PAO.MS154]

**WILSON, CHARLES**, a yeoman from Ireland, settled in Smith, Newcastle, Ontario, on 5 January 1819. [PAO.MS154]

**WILSON, JAMES**, sr., with his wife and two daughters, from County Down, landed from the Alexander on 20 June 1815, settled in Bathurst, Ontario. [PAO.MS154]

**WILSON, JAMES**, jr., from County Down, landed from the Alexander on 20 June 1815, settled in Bathurst, Ontario. [PAO.MS154]

**WILSON, JAMES**, from Ireland, settled in Goulburn, Ontario, on 29 September 1820. [PAO.MS154]

**WILSON, JOHN**, born in Galway around 1696, 5 feet 8 inches tall, a schoolmaster who deserted from Captain Robert Hodgson's Independent Company in 1746. [VaGaz.27.6.1746]

**WILSON, JOHN**, born around 1717, an Irish indentured servant who absconded from Stephen Onion, Gunpowder Iron Works, Maryland, on 24 March 1747. [MdGaz#102]

**WILSON, JOHN**, from Ireland, settled in Cavan, Newcastle, Ontario, on 13 September 1817. [PAO.MS154]

**WILSON, JOHN**, from Ireland, settled in Brock, Home, Ontario, on 11 October 1817. [PAO.MS154]

**WILSON, JOHN**, from Ireland, settled in Beckwith, Ontario, on 29 March 1820. [PAO.MS154]

**WILSON, JOSEPH**, a pewterer, possibly from Dungannon, County Tyrone, settled in Wilmington, Delaware, before 1774. [PRONI#D1044/404]

**WILSON, MOSES,** from Ireland, settled in Huntley, Ontario, on 12 September 1821. [PAO.MS154]

**WILSON, SAMUEL,** from Ireland, settled in Cavan, Newcastle, Ontario, on 10 June 1818. [PAO.MS154]

**WILLSON, THOMAS,** from Ireland, settled in Monaghan, Newcastle, Ontario, on 16 April 1818. [PAO.MS154]

**WILSON, THOMAS,** with his wife, two sons and four daughters, from Ireland, settled in Lanark, Ontario, on 20 March 1821. [PAO.MS154]

**WILSON, WILLIAM,** from Ireland, settled in Beckwith, Ontario, on 29 March 1820. [PAO.MS154]

**WILTON, ROGER,** from Ireland, settled in Huntley, Ontario, on 30 November 1821. [PAO.MS154]

**WILTON, THOMAS,** born in Ireland during 1851, emigrated via Glasgow, Scotland, to Halifax, Nova Scotia, on the SS Manitoban in April 1881. [PANS#C4511]

**WISEMAN, WILLIAM,** with his wife, son and daughter, from Ireland, settled in Lanark, Ontario, on 21 December 1821. [PAO.MS154]

**WITHERS, alias DELANEY, WILLIAM,** born 1722, deserted from the Maryland Forces at Fort Frederick in 1756. [MdGaz#587]

**WOOD, JOSEPH,** and his wife, from Ireland, settled in Lanark, Ontario, on 1 November 1821. [PAO.MS154]

**WOODS, HUGH J.,** from Belfast, married Jessie Matthewson Dobie, daughter of William Cowan Dobie and his wife Agnes Matthewson in Dunfermline, Fife, in Raton, New Mexico, on 18 December 1888, later settled in Kansas City, Missouri. [Dunfermline Journal]

**WOODS, WILLIAM,** son of Sarah Cleland or Woods {1777-1832}, settled in Coldspring, USA. [Kilmore g/s, County Down]

**WOODSIDE, SAMUEL,** probably from the parish of Billy, County Antrim, settled as a bottler in Philadelphia by 1837. [PRONI#d1828/7]

**WOOLEY, REBECCA,** arrived in America 1746, an indentured servant who absconded from George and Richard Lee in Westmoreland County, Virginia, on 21 August 1749. [MdGaz#229]

**WORKMAN, ALEXANDER,** from Ireland, settled in Huntley, Ontario, on 29 November 1821. [PAO.MS154]

**WORKMAN, BENJAMIN,** from Ireland, settled in Huntley, Ontario, on 30 June 1822. [PAO.MS154]

**WORKMAN, ROBERT,** from Ireland, settled in Huntley, Ontario, on 21 May 1821. [PAO.MS154]

**WRAY, JAMES,** from Quilley Colerane, parish of Dunboe, County Londonderry, settled in Spruce Creek, Philadelphia, by 1818. [PRONI#T1727/2]

**WRIGHT, DAVID,** from Dublin to North Carolina on the George of Dublin, master Thomas Cumming, in 1735. [ICJ]

**WRIGHT, ELIZABETH,** from Dublin to North Carolina on the George of Dublin, master Thomas Cumming, in 1735. [ICJ]

**WRIGHT, JAMES,** late of the Royal Sappers, with his wife and three sons, settled in Lanark, Ontario, 1 November 1820. [PAO.MS154]

**WRIGHT, THOMAS,** a Quaker, emigrated from Carlingford on 29 April 1773, landed in Newcastle, Delaware, on 12 June 1773, settled in Plumstead, Bucks County, Pennsylvania, by 1774. [PRONI#D1044/400]

**WRINN, WILLIAM,** an indentured servant who emigrated from Limerick to America on the Industry of Westhaven, master James Lowes, in March 1774. [Hook pp, DU]

**WYLIE, THOMAS,** born 1712, Jane born 1720, Elizabeth born 1748, Henry born 1749, Thomas born 1751, Jane born 1751, Ann born 1758, and Margaret born 1760, arrived in South Carolina in January 1768 on the brigantine Chichester, master William Reid, from Belfast. [SCCJ.34.1]

**WYLY, SAMUEL,** from Dublin to Brunswick, North Carolina, in 1751. [PRONI#D162/52]

**WYNN, RICHARD,** born 1796, emigrated from Cove on the Stakesby to Quebec on 8 July 1823, settled in Ramsay township, Ontario. [PAO.prp]

**YOUNG, BRICE,** settled in Bathurst, Ontario, on 12 December 1821. [PAO.MS154]

**YOUNG, GEORGE,** from Ireland, formerly a private of the 3rd Regiment, settled in Oxford, Ontario, 13 October 1817. [PAO.MS154]

**YOUNG, JAMES,** from Ireland, late a sergeant of the 103$^{rd}$ Regiment, settled in Drummond, Ontario, on 22 June 1822. [PAO.MS154]

**YOUNG, JOHN,** born 1781, with his wife Katherine born 1783, and children Rachel born 1804, Margaret born 1805, Letitia born 1806, Dorah born 1808, Katherine born 1810, Mary Anne born 1818, and Harriet born 1820, from Adare, County Limerick, emigrated from Cove on the Stakesby to Quebec on 8 July 1823, settled in Ramsay township, Ontario. [PAO.prp]

**YOUNG, THOMAS,** from Ireland, landed from the Mary Bell on 8 July 1817, settled in South Crosby, Ontario. [PAO.MS154]

**YOUNG, WILLIAM,** sr., with his wife and son from Ireland, landed from the Mary Bell on 8 July 1817, settled in South Crosby, Ontario, on 4 October 1817. [PAO.MS154]

**YOUNG, WILLIAM,** jr., from Ireland, landed from the Mary Bell on 8 July 1817, settled in South Crosby, Ontario, on 3 October 1817. [PAO.MS154]

# REFERENCES

## Archives

| | | |
|---|---|---|
| CCA | = | Chester County Archives |
| DU | = | Duke University, North Carolina |
| LCHS | = | Lancaster County Historical Society |
| LRO | = | Lancashire Record Office |
| MSA | = | Maryland State Archives |
| NAS | = | National Archives of Scotland |
| NLI | = | National Library of Ireland |
| PAO | = | Public Archives of Ontario |
| PRONI | = | Public Record Office, Northern Ireland |

## Publications

| | | |
|---|---|---|
| BNL | = | Belfast Newsletter, series |
| EC | = | Edinburgh Courant, series |
| GM | = | Gentleman's Magazine, series |
| ICJ | = | Irish Commons Journal, series |
| MdGaz | = | Maryland Gazette, series |
| NYGBR | = | New York Genl. Bio. Rec., series |
| RGG | = | Roll of Graduates of Glasgow, 1727-1897 |
| S | = | Scotsman, series |
| SCCJ | = | South Carolina Council Journal |
| SPDom | = | Cal. State Papers, Domestic, series |
| UF | = | Ulster Folklife, series |
| VaGaz | = | Virginia Gazette, series |
| WHM= | = | Walker's Hibernian Magazine, series |